Stand Out 1

Standards-Based English

Second Edition

Rob Jenkins

Staci Johnson

Australia · Brazil · Japan · Korea · Mexico · Singapore · Spain · United Kingdom · United States

HEINLE
CENGAGE Learning

Stand Out 1: Standards-Based English
Rob Jenkins and Staci Johnson

Publisher: Sherrise Roehr

Acquisitions Editor: Tom Jefferies

Development Editor: Michael Ryall

Director of Content and
Media Production: Michael Burggren

Product Marketing Manager: Katie Kelley

Sr. Content Project Manager: Maryellen E. Killeen

Sr. Print Buyer: Mary Beth Hennebury

Development Editor: Kasia McNabb

Project Manager: Tunde A. Dewey

Cover / Text Designer: Studio Montage

Photo Researcher: Erika Hokanson

Illustrators: James Edwards, Scott McNeill,
S.I. International

Compositor: PrePressPMG

Library of Congress Number: 2008925566

ISBN-13: 978-1-4240-0256-6

ISBN-10: 1-4240-0256-7

ISE ISBN: 1-4240-1905-2

Cengage Learning
25 Thomson Place
Boston, MA 02210
USA

Cengage Learning is a leading provider of customized learning solutions with office locations around the globe, including Singapore, the United Kingdom, Australia, Mexico, Brazil, and Japan. Locate your local office at:
international.cengage.com/region

Cengage Learning products are represented in Canada by Nelson Education, Ltd.

Visit Heinle online at **elt.heinle.com**
Visit our corporate website at **cengage.com**

Printed in Canada
4 5 6 7 11

ACKNOWLEDGMENTS

Elizabeth Aderman
New York City Board of Education, New York, NY

Sharon Baker
Roseville Adult School, Roseville, CA

Lillian Barredo
Stockton School for Adults, Stockton, CA

Linda Boice
Elk Grove Adult Education, Elk Grove, CA

Chan Bostwick
Los Angeles Unified School District, Los Angeles, CA

Debra Brooks
Manhattan BEGIN Program, New York, NY

Anne Byrnes
North Hollywood-Polytechnic Community Adult School, Sun Valley, CA

Rose Cantu
John Jay High School, San Antonio, TX

Toni Chapralis
Fremont School for Adults, Sacramento, CA

Melanie Chitwood
Miami-Dade College, Miami, FL

Geri Creamer
Stockton School for Adults, Stockton, CA

Stephanie Daubar
Harry W. Brewster Technical Center, Tampa, FL

Irene Dennis
San Antonio College, San Antonio, TX

Eileen Duffell
P.S. 64, New York, NY

Nancy Dunlap
Northside Independent School District, San Antonio, TX

Gloria Eriksson
Grant Skills Center, Sacramento, CA

Marti Estrin
Santa Rosa Junior College, Santa Rosa, CA

Lawrence Fish
Shorefront YM-YWHA English Language Program, Brooklyn, NY

Victoria Florit
Miami-Dade College, Miami, FL

Rhoda Gilbert
New York City Board of Education, New York, NY

Kathleen Jimenez
Miami-Dade College, Miami, FL

Nancy Jordan
John Jay High School Adult Education, San Antonio, TX

Renee Klosz
Lindsey Hopkins Technical Education Center, Miami, FL

David Lauter
Stockton School for Adults, Stockton, CA

Patricia Long
Old Marshall Adult Education Center, Sacramento, CA

Daniel Loos
Seattle Community College, Seattle, WA

Maria Miranda
Lindsey Hopkins Technical Education Center, Miami, FL

Karen Moore
Stockton School for Adults, Stockton, CA

George Myskiw
Malcolm X College, Chicago, IL

Heidi Perez
Lawrence Public Schools Adult Learning Center, Lawrence, MA

Marta Pitt
Lindsey Hopkins Technical Education Center, Miami, FL

Sylvia Rambach
Stockton School for Adults, Stockton, CA

Eric Rosenbaum
BEGIN Managed Programs, New York, NY

Laura Rowley
Old Marshall Adult Education Center, Sacramento, CA

Stephanie Schmitter
Mercer County Community College, Trenton, NJ

Amy Schneider
Pacoima Skills Center, Pacoima, CA

Sr. M. B. Theresa Spittle
Stockton School for Adults, Stockton, CA

Andre Sutton
Belmont Adult School, Los Angeles, CA

Jennifer Swoyer
Northside Independent School District, San Antonio, TX

Claire Valier
Palm Beach County School District, West Palm Beach, FL

Rob Jenkins

Staci Johnson

I love teaching. I love to see the expressions on my students' faces when the light goes on and their eyes show such sincere joy of learning. I knew the first time I stepped into an ESL classroom that this was where I needed to be and I have never questioned that resolution. I have worked in business, sales, and publishing, and I've found challenge in all, but nothing can compare to the satisfaction of reaching people in such a personal way.

Ever since I can remember, I've been fascinated with other cultures and languages. I love to travel and every place I go, the first thing I want to do is meet the people, learn their language, and understand their culture. Becoming an ESL teacher was a perfect way to turn what I love to do into my profession. There's nothing more incredible than the exchange of teaching and learning from one another that goes on in an ESL classroom. And there's nothing more rewarding than helping a student succeed.

We are so happy that instructors and agencies have embraced the lesson planning and project-based activities that we introduced in the first edition and are so enthusiastically teaching with **Stand Out**. It is fantastic that so many of our colleagues are as excited to be in this profession as we are. After writing over 500 lesson plans and implementing them in our own classrooms and after personal discussions with thousands of instructors all over the United States and in different parts of the world, we have found ourselves in a position to improve upon our successful model. One of the most notable things in the new edition is that we have continued to stress integrating skills in each lesson and have made this integration more apparent and obvious. To accomplish any life skill, students need to incorporate a combination of reading, writing, listening, speaking, grammar, pronunciation, and academic skills while developing vocabulary and these skills should be taught together in a lesson! We have accomplished this by extending the presentation of lessons in the book, so each lesson is more fully developed. You will also notice an extended list of ancillaries and a tighter correlation of these ancillaries to each book. The ancillaries allow you to extend practice on particular skill areas beyond the lesson in the text. We are so excited about this curriculum and know that as you implement it, you and your students will *stand out*.

Our goal is to give students
challenging opportunities
to be successful in their
language-learning experience
so they develop confidence
and become independent,
lifelong learners.

Rob Jenkins
Staci Johnson

ABOUT THE SERIES

The **Stand Out** series is designed to facilitate *active* learning while challenging students to build a nurturing and effective learning community.

The student books are divided into eight distinct units, mirroring competency areas most useful to newcomers. These areas are outlined in CASAS assessment programs and different state model standards for adults. Each unit in *Stand Out 1* is then divided into five lessons, a review, and a team project. Lessons are driven by performance objectives and are filled with challenging activities that progress from teacher-presented to student-centered tasks.

SUPPLEMENTAL MATERIALS

- The *Stand Out 1 Lesson Planner* is in full color with 60 complete lesson plans, taking the instructor through each stage of a lesson from warm-up and review through application.
- The *Stand Out 1 Activity Bank CD-ROM* has an abundance of customizable worksheets. Print or download and modify what you need for your particular class.
- The *Stand Out 1 Grammar Challenge* is a workbook that gives additional grammar explanation and practice in context.
- The *Reading and Writing Challenge* workbooks are designed to capture the principle ideas in the student book, and allow students to improve their vocabulary, academic, reading, and writing skills.
- The *Stand Out 1 Assessment CD-ROM with ExamView®* allows you to customize pre- and post-tests for each unit as well as a pre- and post-test for the book.
- Listening scripts are found in the back of the student book and in the Lesson Planner. CDs are available with focused listening activities described in the Lesson Planner.

STAND OUT 1 LESSON PLANNER

The *Stand Out 1 Lesson Planner* is a new and innovative approach. As many seasoned teachers know, good lesson planning can make a substantial difference in the classroom. Students continue coming to class, understanding, applying, and remembering more of what they learn. They are more confident in their learning when good lesson planning techniques are incorporated.

We have developed lesson plans that are designed to be used each day and to reduce preparation time. The planner includes:

- Standard lesson progression (Warm-up and Review, Introduction, Presentation, Practice, Evaluation, and Application)

- A creative and complete way to approach varied class lengths so that each lesson will work within a class period.
- 180 hours of classroom activities
- Time suggestions for each activity
- Pedagogical comments
- Space for teacher notes and future planning
- Identification of LCP standards in addition to SCANS and CASAS standards

USER QUESTIONS ABOUT STAND OUT

- **What are SCANS and EFF and how do they integrate into the book?**
  SCANS is the Secretary's Commission on Achieving Necessary Skills. SCANS was developed to encourage students to prepare for the workplace. The standards developed through SCANS have been incorporated throughout the **Stand Out** student books and components.

  Stand Out addresses SCANS a little differently than do other books. SCANS standards elicit effective teaching strategies by incorporating essential skills such as critical thinking and group work. We have incorporated SCANS standards in every lesson, not isolating these standards in the work unit. All new texts have followed our lead.

  EFF, or Equipped For the Future, is another set of standards established to address students' roles as parents, workers, and citizens, with a vision of student literacy and lifelong learning. **Stand Out** addresses these standards and integrates them into the materials in a similar way to SCANS.

- **What about CASAS?** The federal government has mandated that states show student outcomes as a prerequisite to receiving funding. Some states have incorporated the **C**omprehensive **A**dult **S**tudent **A**ssessment **S**ystem (CASAS) testing to standardize agency reporting. Unfortunately, many of our students are unfamiliar with standardized testing and therefore struggle with it. Adult schools need to develop lesson plans to address specific concerns. **Stand Out** was developed with careful attention to CASAS skill areas in most lessons and performance objectives.

- **Are the tasks too challenging for my students?** Students learn by doing and learn more when challenged. **Stand Out** provides tasks that encourage critical thinking in a variety of ways. The tasks in each lesson move from teacher-directed to student-centered so the learner clearly understands what's expected and is willing to "take a risk." The lessons are expected to be challenging. In this way, students learn that when they work together as a learning community, anything becomes possible. The satisfaction of accomplishing something both as an individual and as a member of a team results in greater confidence and effective learning.

- **Do I need to understand lesson planning to teach from the student book?** If you don't understand lesson planning when you start, you will when you finish! Teaching from **Stand Out** is like a course on lesson planning, especially if you use the Lesson Planner on a daily basis.

  Stand Out does *stand out* because, when we developed this series, we first established performance objectives for each lesson. Then we designed lesson plans, followed by student book pages. The introduction to each lesson varies because different objectives demand different approaches. **Stand Out's** variety of tasks makes learning more interesting for the student.

- **What are team projects?** The final lesson of each unit is a **team project**. This is often a team simulation that incorporates the objectives of the unit and provides an additional opportunity for students to actively apply what they have learned. The project allows students to produce something that represents their progress in learning. These end-of-unit projects were created with a variety of learning styles and individual skills in mind. The team projects can be skipped or simplified, but we encourage instructors to implement them, enriching the overall student experience.

- **What do you mean by a customizable Activity Bank?** Every class, student, teacher, and approach is different. Since no one textbook can meet all these differences, the *Stand Out Activity Bank CD-ROM* allows you to customize **Stand Out** for your class. You can copy different activities and worksheets from the CD-ROM to your hard drive and then:

  - change items in supplemental vocabulary, grammar, and life skill activities;
  - personalize activities with student names and popular locations in your area;
  - extend every lesson with additional practice where you feel it is most needed.

  The Activity Bank also includes the following resources:

  - Multilevel worksheets – worksheets based on the standard worksheets described above, but at one level higher and one level lower.

  - Graphic organizer templates – templates that can be used to facilitate learning. They include graphs, charts, VENN diagrams, and so on.

- Computer worksheets – worksheets designed to supplement each unit and progress from simple to complex operations in word processing; and spreadsheets for labs and computer enhanced classrooms.

- Internet worksheets – worksheets designed to supplement each unit and provide application opportunities beyond the lessons in the book.

- **Is *Stand Out* grammar-based or competency-based?** **Stand Out** is a competency-based series; however, students are exposed to basic grammar structures. We believe that grammar instruction in context is extremely important. Grammar is a necessary component for achieving most competencies; therefore it is integrated into most lessons. Students are first provided with context that incorporates the grammar, followed by an explanation and practice. At this level, we expect students to learn basic structures, but we do not expect them to acquire them. It has been our experience that students are exposed several times within their learning experience to language structures before they actually acquire them. For teachers who want to enhance grammar instruction, the *Activity Bank CD-ROM* and/or the *Grammar Challenge* workbooks provide ample opportunities.

  The six competencies that drive **Stand Out** are basic communication, consumer economics, community resources, health, occupational knowledge, and lifelong learning (government and law replace lifelong learning in Books 3 and 4).

- **Are there enough activities so I don't have to supplement?** **Stand Out** stands alone in providing 180 hours of instruction and activities, even without the additional suggestions in the Lesson Planner. The Lesson Planner also shows you how to streamline lessons to provide 90 hours of classwork and still have thorough lessons if you meet less often. When supplementing with the *Stand Out Activity Bank CD-ROM*, the *Assessment CD-ROM with ExamView®* and the *Stand Out Grammar Challenge* workbook, you gain unlimited opportunities to extend class hours and provide activities related directly to each lesson objective. Calculate how many hours your class meets in a semester and look to **Stand Out** to address the full class experience.

  Stand Out is a comprehensive approach to adult language learning, meeting needs of students and instructors completely and effectively.

CONTENTS

• Grammar points that are explicitly taught   ◊ Grammar points that are presented in context   △ Grammar points that are being recycled

	Numeracy/ Academic Skills	EFF	SCANS	CASAS
Pre-Unit	• Clarification strategies • Pronunciation • Focused listening	• Speaking so others can understand • Listening actively	• Listening • Speaking • Sociability	**1:** 0.1.1, 0.1.4, 0.2.1 **2:** 0.1.2, 0.1.4, 0.2.2 **3:** 0.1.5, 0.1.6, 2.2.1
Unit 1	• Focused listening • Predicting • Reviewing • Self-evaluation	Most EFF skills are incorporated into this unit, with an emphasis on: • Conveying ideas in writing • Taking responsibility for learning • Reflecting and evaluating (Technology is optional.)	Most SCANS are incorporated into this unit, with an emphasis on: • Acquiring information • Interpreting and evaluating information • Writing (Technology is optional.)	**1:** 0.1.2, 0.2.1 **2:** 0.1.2, 0.1.3, 1.1.4 **3:** 0.1.2 **4:** 0.2.4 **5:** 2.3.1 **R:** 0.1.2, 0.1.3, 0.2.1, 0.2.4, 1.1.4, 2.3.1, 4.8.1 **TP:** 0.1.2, 0.1.3, 0.2.1, 0.2.4, 1.1.4, 2.3.1
Unit 2	• Categorizing • Classifying • Focused listening • Graphs • Predicting • Reviewing • Self-evaluation	Most EFF skills are incorporated into this unit, with an emphasis on: • Using mathematics in problem solving and communication • Solving problems and making decisions • Reflecting and evaluating (Technology is optional.)	Most SCANS are incorporated into this unit, with an emphasis on: • Allocating money • Serving customers • Organizing and maintaining information • Decision making (Technology is optional.)	**1:** 1.1.3, 1.3.7, 2.5.4 **2:** 1.3.3, 1.3.8, 1.3.9, 1.6.4 **3:** 1.2.1, 1.3.9 **4:** 1.3.9 **5:** 0.1.2, 1.1.9, 1.3.9 **R:** 0.1.2, 1.1.9, 1.2.1, 1.3.3, 1.3.8, 1.3.9, 1.6.4 **TP:** 0.1.2, 1.1.9, 1.2.1, 1.3.3, 1.3.8, 1.3.9, 1.6.4, 4.8.1

Contents

CONTENTS

● Grammar points that are explicitly taught   ◊ Grammar points that are presented in context   △ Grammar points that are being recycled

	Numeracy/ Academic Skills	EFF	SCANS	CASAS
Unit 3	• Brainstorming • Classifying • Critical thinking • Focused listening • Making graphs • Predicting • Reviewing • Self-evaluation	Most EFF skills are incorporated into this unit, with an emphasis on: • Using mathematics in problem solving and communication • Learning through research. (Technology is optional.)	Most SCANS are incorporated into this unit, with an emphasis on: • Allocating money • Understanding systems • Creative thinking • Seeing things in the mind's eye (Technology is optional.)	**1:** 1.3.8, 7.2.3 **2:** 1.2.1, 1.2.4, 1.3.8 **3:** 0.1.2, 1.1.7, 1.3.8, 7.2.6 **4:** 1.1.3, 1.2.1, 1.2.2, 1.3.8 **5:** 1.3.8, 2.6.4, 7.2.3 **R:** 0.1.2, 1.1.3, 1.1.7, 1.2.1, 1.2.2, 1.2.4, 2.6.4 **TP:** 0.1.2, 1.1.3, 1.1.7, 1.2.1, 1.2.2, 1.2.4, 2.6.4, 4.8.1
Unit 4	• Classifying • Focused listening • Pie charts • Reviewing • Self-evaluation • Venn diagrams	Most EFF skills are incorporated into this unit, with an emphasis on: • Using mathematics in problem solving and communication • Solving problems and making decisions • Reflecting and evaluating (Technology is optional.)	Most SCANS are incorporated into this unit, with an emphasis on: • Acquiring and evaluating information • Creative thinking • Seeing things in the mind's eye (Technology is optional.)	**1:** 1.1.3, 1.4.1 **2:** 1.1.3, 1.4.1, 4.8.1, 7.2.3 **3:** 1.4.2 **4:** 1.4.2 **5:** 1.4.1, 1.4.2, 2.2.1 **R:** 1.4.1, 1.4.2 **TP:** 1.4.1, 1.4.2, 4.8.1
Unit 5	• Brainstorming • Classifying • Focused listening • Reviewing • Scanning for information • Self-evaluation	Most EFF skills are incorporated into this unit, with an emphasis on: • Reading with understanding • Solving problems and making decisions • Learning through research (Technology is optional.)	Most SCANS are incorporated into this unit, with an emphasis on: • Acquiring and evaluating information • Reading • Seeing things in the mind's eye • Sociability (Technology is optional.)	**1:** 1.1.3, 2.5.1, 2.5.3, 7.4.4 **2:** 1.1.3, 1.9.1, 1.9.4, 2.2.1, 2.2.2, 2.2.5 **3:** 1.3.7, 2.2.1, 2.5.4 **4:** 2.1.7, 2.1.8 **5:** 0.2.3 **R:** 0.2.3, 1.1.3, 2.1.7, 2.1.8, 1.9.1, 2.2.2 **TP:** 0.2.3, 1.1.3, 2.1.7, 2.1.8, 1.9.1, 2.2.2, 4.8.1

CONTENTS

• Grammar points that are explicitly taught   ◊ Grammar points that are presented in context   ∆ Grammar points that are being recycled

	Numeracy/ Academic Skills	EFF	SCANS	CASAS
Unit 6	• Clarification strategies • Focused listening • Graphs • Predicting • Ranking • Reviewing • Self-evaluation • VENN diagrams	Most EFF skills are incorporated into this unit, with an emphasis on: • Solving problems and making decisions • Reflecting and evaluating • Learning through research (Technology is optional.)	Most SCANS are incorporated into this unit, with an emphasis on: • Interpreting and communicating information • Understanding systems • Decision making (Technology is optional.)	**1:** 3.1.1 **2:** 3.1.1, 6.6.5 **3:** 0.1.3, 3.3.1, 3.3.2, 3.3.3 **4:** 0.1.2, 2.5.1 **5:** 1.1.3, 3.5.9, 7.1.1 **R:** 2.5.1, 3.1.1, 3.3.1, 3.3.2, 3.3.3, 3.5.9 **TP:** 2.5.1, 3.1.1, 3.3.1, 3.3.2, 3.3.3, 3.5.9, 4.8.1
Unit 7	• Clarification strategies • Classifying • Focused listening • Peer editing • Ranking • Reviewing • Scanning • Self-evaluation • VENN diagrams	Most EFF skills are incorporated into this unit, with an emphasis on: • Solving problems and making decisions • Learning through research (Technology is optional.)	Most SCANS are incorporated into this unit, with an emphasis on: • Organizing and maintaining information • Understanding systems • Creative thinking • Decision making (Technology is optional.)	**1:** 4.1.8 **2:** 4.1.3, 4.1.6, 4.1.8 **3:** 4.1.2, 4.1.8 **4:** 0.1.1, 0.1.6, 4.1.5, 4.6.1 **5:** 4.4.1, 4.4.4 **R:** 4.1.2, 4.1.3, 4.1.6, 4.1.8, 4.1.5, 4.4.1, 4.4.4, 4.6.1 **TP:** 4.1.2, 4.1.3, 4.1.6, 4.1.8, 4.1.5, 4.4.1, 4.4.4, 4.6.1, 4.8.1
Unit 8	• Focused listening • Note-taking • Organizational strategies • Predicting • Reviewing • Self-evaluation	Most EFF skills are incorporated into this unit, with an emphasis on: • Planning • Taking responsibility for learning • Reflecting and evaluating (Technology is optional.)	Most SCANS are incorporated into this unit, with an emphasis on: • Understanding systems • Monitoring and correcting performance • Knowing how to learn • Self-management (Technology is optional.)	**1:** 7.4.1 **2:** 7.1.4, 7.4.1, 7.4.9 **3:** 2.5.5, 7.1.1 **4:** 7.1.1, 7.5.1 **5:** 7.1.1, 7.1.2 **R:** 7.1.1, 7.1.4, 7.4.1, 7.4.9, 7.5.1 **TP:** 4.8.1, 7.1.1, 7.1.4, 7.4.1, 7.4.9, 7.5.1

Welcome to Stand Out, Second Edition

Stand Out works.

And now it works even better!

Built from the standards necessary for adult English learners, the second edition of *Stand Out* gives students the foundation and tools they need to develop confidence and become independent, lifelong learners.

- **Pronunciation** activities are integrated through the program.

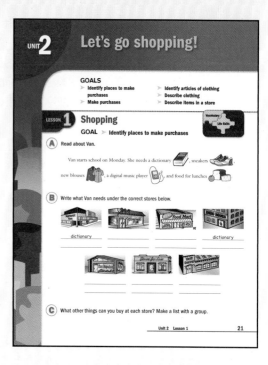

- Clearly defined **goals** provide a roadmap of learning for the student.
- State and federally required **life skills and competencies** are taught, helping students meet necessary benchmarks.
- Key **vocabulary** is introduced visually and orally.

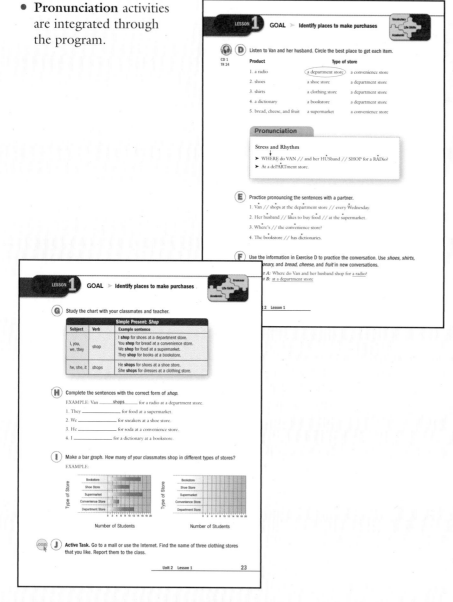

- Activities involving **academic skills** increase students' ability to navigate through the academic classroom.

- A variety of **examples from real life**, like bank checks, newspaper ads, maps, etc. help students learn to access information and resources in their community.

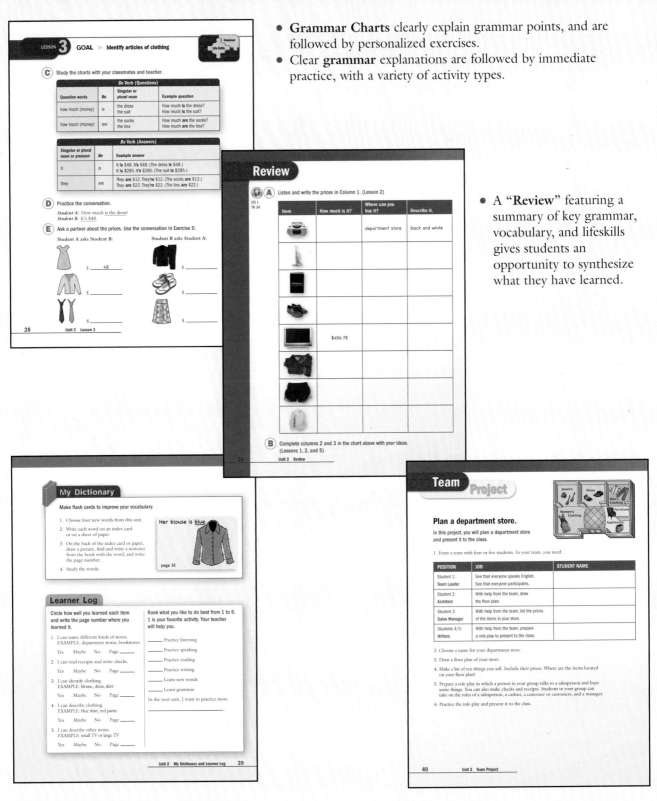

- **Grammar Charts** clearly explain grammar points, and are followed by personalized exercises.
- Clear **grammar** explanations are followed by immediate practice, with a variety of activity types.

- A **"Review"** featuring a summary of key grammar, vocabulary, and lifeskills gives students an opportunity to synthesize what they have learned.

- **"My Dictionary"** activity allows learners to use the vocabulary from the unit in a new way, increasing the likelihood that they will acquire the words.
- **"Learner Log"** provides opportunities for learner self-assessment.

- **"Team Projects"** present motivating cross-ability activities which group learners of different levels together to complete a task that applies the unit objective.

The ground-breaking *Stand Out* **Lesson Planners** take the guesswork out of meeting the standards while offering high-interest, meaningful language activities, and three levels of pacing for each book.

- An **at-a-glance prep** and **agenda section** for each lesson ensure that instructors have a clear knowledge of what will be covered in the lesson.

- A complete **lesson plan** for each page in the student book is provided, following a standard lesson progression (Warm-up and Review, Introduction, Presentation, Practice, Evaluation, and Application).

- Clear, easy-to-identify **pacing guide** icons offer three different pacing strategies.

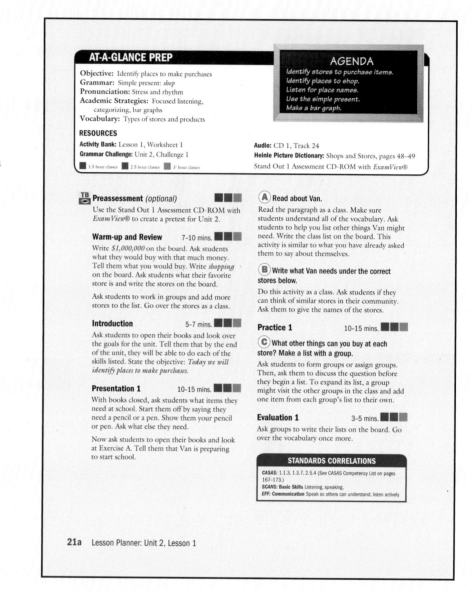

AT-A-GLANCE PREP

Objective: Identify places to make purchases
Grammar: Simple present: *shop*
Pronunciation: Stress and rhythm
Academic Strategies: Focused listening, categorizing, bar graphs
Vocabulary: Types of stores and products

RESOURCES

Activity Bank: Lesson 1, Worksheet 1
Grammar Challenge: Unit 2, Challenge 1

Audio: CD 1, Track 24
Heinle Picture Dictionary: Shops and Stores, pages 48–49
Stand Out 1 Assessment CD-ROM with *ExamView®*

■ 1.5 hour classes ■ 2.5 hour classes ■ 3+ hour classes

AGENDA
Identify stores to purchase items.
Identify places to shop.
Listen for place names.
Use the simple present.
Make a bar graph.

Preassessment *(optional)* ■■■
Use the Stand Out 1 Assessment CD-ROM with *ExamView®* to create a pretest for Unit 2.

Warm-up and Review 7–10 mins. ■■■
Write *$1,000,000* on the board. Ask students what they would buy with that much money. Tell them what you would buy. Write *shopping* on the board. Ask students what their favorite store is and write the stores on the board.

Ask students to work in groups and add more stores to the list. Go over the stores as a class.

Introduction 5–7 mins. ■■■
Ask students to open their books and look over the goals for the unit. Tell them that by the end of the unit, they will be able to do each of the skills listed. State the objective: *Today we will identify places to make purchases.*

Presentation 1 10–15 mins. ■■■
With books closed, ask students what items they need at school. Start them off by saying they need a pencil or a pen. Show them your pencil or pen. Ask what else they need.

Now ask students to open their books and look at Exercise A. Tell them that Van is preparing to start school.

(A) Read about Van.
Read the paragraph as a class. Make sure students understand all of the vocabulary. Ask students to help you list other things Van might need. Write the class list on the board. This activity is similar to what you have already asked them to say about themselves.

(B) Write what Van needs under the correct stores below.
Do this activity as a class. Ask students if they can think of similar stores in their community. Ask them to give the names of the stores.

Practice 1 10–15 mins. ■■■
(C) What other things can you buy at each store? Make a list with a group.
Ask students to form groups or assign groups. Then, ask them to discuss the question before they begin a list. To expand its list, a group might visit the other groups in the class and add one item from each group's list to their own.

Evaluation 1 3–5 mins. ■■■
Ask groups to write their lists on the board. Go over the vocabulary once more.

STANDARDS CORRELATIONS

CASAS: 1.1.3, 1.3.7, 2.5.4 (See CASAS Competency List on pages 167–173.)
SCANS: Basic Skills Listening, speaking,
EFF: Communication Speak so others can understand, listen actively

21a Lesson Planner: Unit 2, Lesson 1

- **"Teaching Tips"** provide ideas and strategies for the classroom.
- Additional **supplemental activities** found on the *Activity Bank CD-ROM* are suggested at their point of use.
- The *Activity Bank CD-ROM* includes **reproducible multilevel activity masters** for each lesson that can be printed or downloaded and modified for classroom needs.
- **"Listening Scripts"** from the *Audio CD* are included.
- **"Standards Correlations"** appear directly on the page, detailing how *Stand Out* meets CASAS, EFF, and SCANS standards.

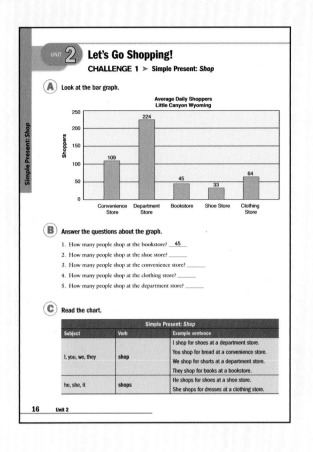

- *Grammar Challenge* workbooks include supplemental activities for students who desire even more contextual grammar and vocabulary practice.
- Clear and concise **grammar explanation boxes** provide a strong foundation for the activities.

- A variety of **activities** allow students develop their grammar skills and apply them.
- Written by **Rob Jenkins** and **Staci Johnson**, the *Grammar Challenge* workbooks are directly aligned to the student books.

- *Reading & Writing Challenge* workbooks are also available. These workbooks provide challenging materials and exercises for students who want even more practice in reading, vocabulary development, and writing.

Welcome to Our Class

GOALS
➤ Greet your friends
➤ Say and write numbers
➤ Follow classroom instructions

LESSON 1

Hello!

GOAL ➤ Greet your friends

Vocabulary · Grammar · Life Skills · Academic · Pronunciation

CD 1
TR 1

A Listen.

Hi!

Hello!

Welcome to our class.

How are you?

Fine! How are you?

GOAL ➤ **Greet your friends**

B **Complete the conversations and practice them with a partner.**

1. *Felipe:* _____. Welcome to our class.
   Student: Hello. Thank you.

2. *Gabriela:* Hi! How _____ ?
   Duong: Fine. _____ ?

3. *Eva:* _____. Welcome to our class.
   Student: Hi. Thank you.

C **Read the greetings.**

hi	hello	welcome	How are you?
good morning	good afternoon	good evening	

  D **Listen and complete the conversation.**

CD 1
TR 2

Roberto: Hi. I'm Roberto. _____ ?

Gabriela: _____. My name is Gabriela. I'm fine, thanks.

Roberto: _____ to our class.

Gabriela: Thank you.

Roberto: Our teacher is Miss Smith.

E Listen and repeat.

CD 1
TR 3

Hi! I'm Gabriela.
G-A-B-R-I-E-L-A.

Hello. I'm Duong.
D-U-O-N-G.

F Listen and repeat.

CD 1
TR 4

Aa	Bb	Cc	Dd	Ee	Ff
Gg	Hh	Ii	Jj	Kk	Ll
Mm	Nn	Oo	Pp	Qq	Rr
Ss	Tt	Uu	Vv	Ww	Xx
Yy	Zz				

Pronunciation

/m/   *I'm*

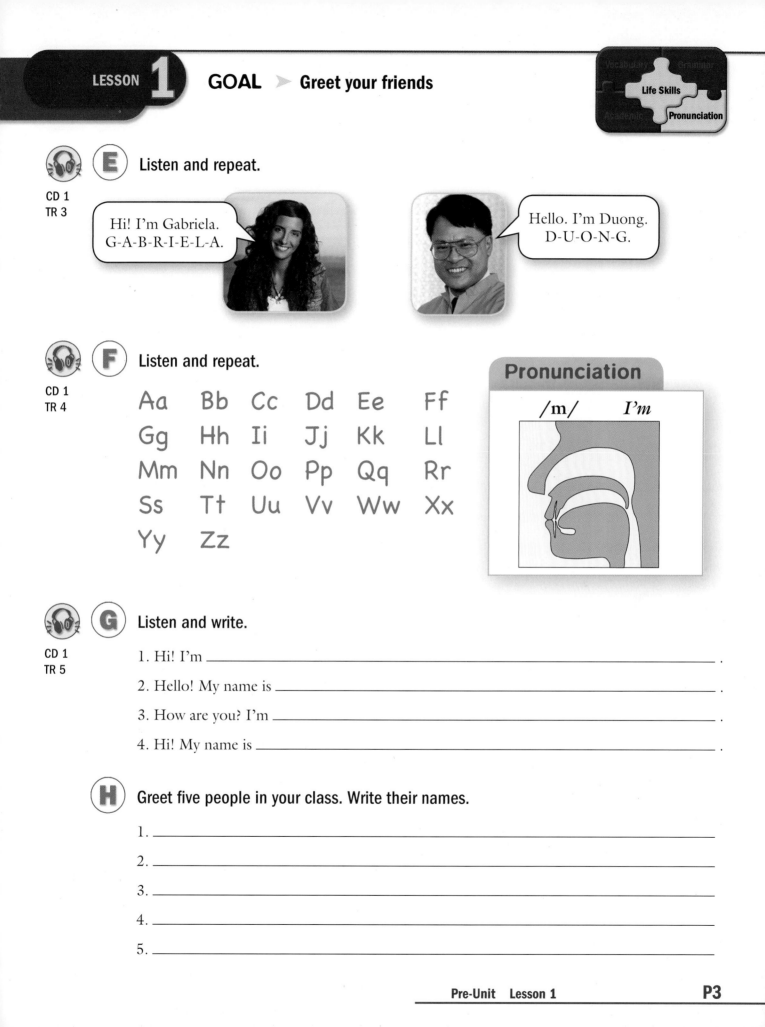

G Listen and write.

CD 1
TR 5

1. Hi! I'm _____ .

2. Hello! My name is _____ .

3. How are you? I'm _____ .

4. Hi! My name is _____ .

H Greet five people in your class. Write their names.

1. _____

2. _____

3. _____

4. _____

5. _____

What's your number?

GOAL ➤ Say and write numbers

What do you see in the picture?
How many students are there?
Where is the teacher?

A Read the paragraph. Circle the numbers.

Welcome to Miss Smith's class. There are 12 students in the class. The students study for 6 hours every week. The school address is 19 Lincoln Street, Los Angeles, California 90011.

B Complete the chart about your class.

Teacher's name	
Number of students	
Number of hours	
Zip code	

GOAL ➤ **Say and write numbers**

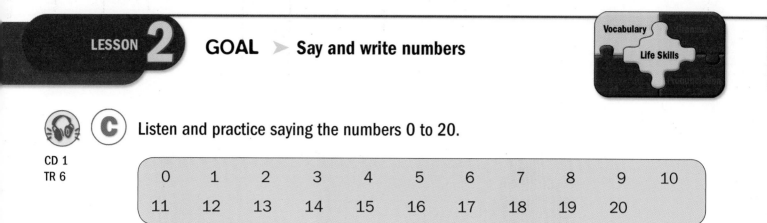

C Listen and practice saying the numbers 0 to 20.

CD 1
TR 6

0	1	2	3	4	5	6	7	8	9	10
11	12	13	14	15	16	17	18	19	20	

D Listen and write the numbers you hear.

CD 1
TR 7

1. _____

2. _____

3. _____

4. _____

5. _____

6. _____

E Listen and write the missing numbers.

CD 1
TR 8

My name is Gabriela. My address is

_____ Main Street. The zip

code is _____. My phone

number is _____. There are

_____ students in my class.

GOAL ➤ **Say and write numbers**

 Read about Gabriela and Eva.

Name: Gabriela Ramirez
Address: 14 Main Street
Zip code: 06119
Phone: 401-555-7248

Name: Eva Malinska
Address: 333 Western Circle
Zip code: 06119
Phone: 401-555-3534

G **Look at the numbers. Write the information in the chart.**

~~2945 Broadway~~	916-555-2386	415-555-7869	72643
800-555-2675	9235 Sundry Way	98724	8 Palm Circle
213-555-5761	78231	9921 Johnson Street	23145

Address	Zip code	Phone
2945 Broadway		

H **Write the numbers. Say the numbers to your partner. Listen and write your partner's numbers.**

	You	Your partner
1. The number of people in your family	_____	_____
2. Your phone number	_____	_____
3. Your address	_____	_____
4. Your zip code	_____	_____

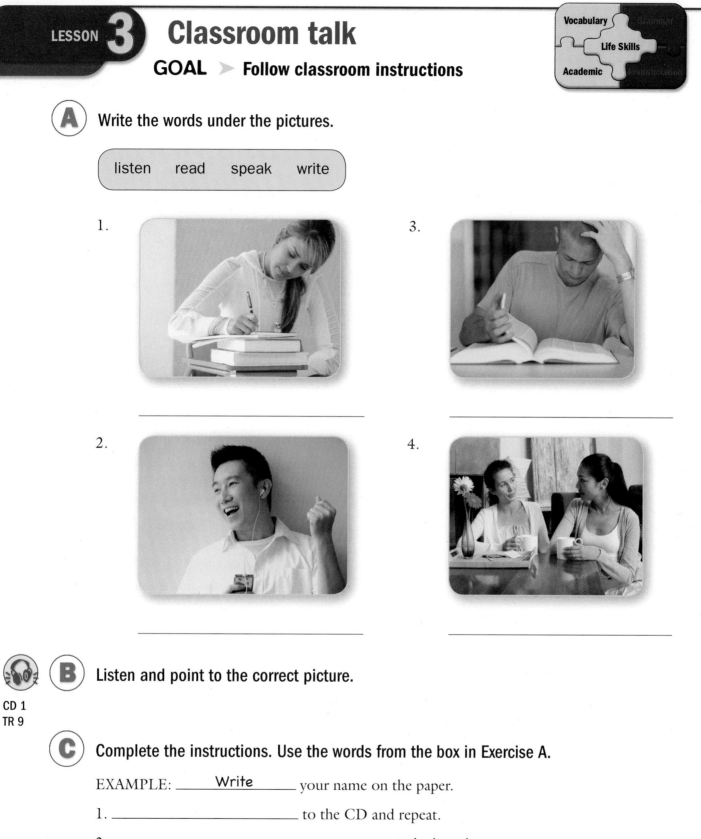

LESSON 3 Classroom talk

GOAL ➤ **Follow classroom instructions**

A Write the words under the pictures.

| listen   read   speak   write |

1.

3.

_____

_____

2.

4.

_____

_____

B Listen and point to the correct picture.

CD 1
TR 9

C Complete the instructions. Use the words from the box in Exercise A.

EXAMPLE: _____Write_____ your name on the paper.

1. _____ to the CD and repeat.

2. _____ your answers on the board.

3. _____ the story and answer the questions.

4. _____ with your partner about the picture.

D **Match the sentences with the pictures. Write the letter.**

___d___ 1. Please stand up.

_____ 2. Please read.

_____ 3. Please sit down.

_____ 4. Please take out a sheet of paper.

_____ 5. Please open your book.

_____ 6. Please listen carefully.

_____ 7. Please write.

_____ 8. Please help Juana.

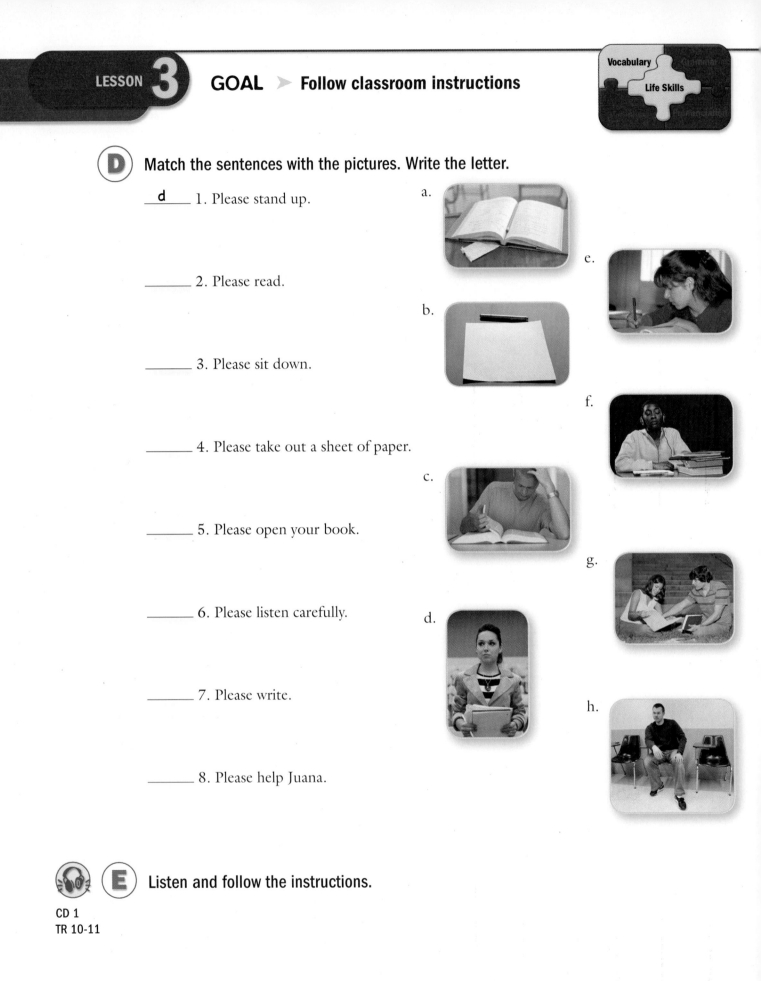

a.

b.

c.

d.

e.

f.

g.

h.

E **Listen and follow the instructions.**

CD 1
TR 10-11

F Read the conversation.

Teacher: Please open your books to page fifteen.
Student: What page?
Teacher: Page fifteen. That's one, five.
Student: Thank you.

G Practice with a partner.

Student B's book is closed.
Student A says:

1. Please open your book to page six.
2. Please open your book to page fourteen.
3. Please open your book to page sixteen.
4. Please open your book to page eight.
5. Please open your book to page nine.
6. Please open your book to page twenty.

H Practice with a partner.

Student A's book is closed.
Student B says:

1. Please open your book to page three.
2. Please open your book to page twelve.
3. Please open your book to page eleven.
4. Please open your book to page four.
5. Please open your book to page seventeen.
6. Please open your book to page nineteen.

I Give instructions to a partner.

1. Please stand up.
2. Please take out your book and open to page fifteen.
3. Please sit down.
4. Please write my name on a sheet of paper.
5. Please read my name.

My Dictionary

Make flash cards to improve your vocabulary.

1. Choose four new words from this unit.

2. Write each word on an index card or on a sheet of paper.

3. On the back of the index card or paper, draw a picture, find and write a sentence from the book with the word, and write the page number.

4. Study the words.

phone

Gabriela's phone number is 401-555-7248.

page P6

Learner Log

Circle how well you learned each item and write the page number where you learned it.

1. I can say *I'm* _____ (your name).

   Yes   Maybe   No   Page _____

2. I can say *hello, hi,* and other greetings.

   Yes   Maybe   No   Page _____

3. I can say and write phone numbers, addresses, and zip codes.

   Yes   Maybe   No   Page _____

4. I can follow instructions.

   Yes   Maybe   No   Page _____

Rank what you like to do best from 1 to 6. 1 is your favorite activity. Your teacher will help you.

_____ Practice listening

_____ Practice speaking

_____ Practice reading

_____ Practice writing

_____ Learn new words

_____ Learn grammar

In the next unit, I want to practice more

_____ .

UNIT 1

Talking with Others

GOALS
➤ Give personal information
➤ Describe people
➤ Describe family relationships
➤ Express preferences
➤ Plan a study schedule

LESSON 1

Where are you from?

GOAL ➤ Give personal information

Where is Roberto from?

A Read about Roberto.

My name is <u>Roberto Garcia</u>. I'm a new student in this school. I'm from <u>Mexico City, Mexico</u>. I'm <u>43</u> years old and I'm <u>married</u>. I'm very happy in my new class.

B Write the underlined words from Exercise A on the correct line.

Name: ___Roberto Garcia_____

Country: _____

Age: _____

Marital status: _____

Vocabulary
Life Skills
Academic

C **Look at the pictures.**

single   married   divorced

 D **Listen and complete the missing information.**

CD 1
TR 12–14

1.

Name: __Eva Malinska__

Age: _____

Marital status: _____

Country: _____

2.

Name: __Gabriela Ramirez__

Age: _____

Marital status: _____

Country: _____

3.

Name: __Felipe Rodriguez__

Age: _____

Marital status: _____

Country: _____

E **Match the questions with the answers. Draw lines.**

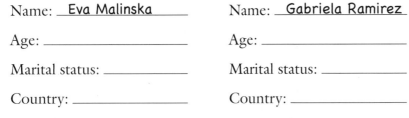

1. Where are you from?   a. Yes, I'm married.

2. What's your name?   b. I'm from Mexico.

3. Are you married?   c. I'm 43 years old.

4. How old are you?   d. Roberto.

F   Study the chart with your classmates and teacher.

Simple Present: *Be*			
Subject	***Be***	**Information**	**Example sentence**
I	am	43 years old	I **am** 43 years old.
he, she	is	single	He **is** single. (Roberto **is** single.)
we, you, they	are	from Argentina	She **is** from Argentina. (Gabriela **is** from Argentina.)
		single	We **are** single.
		married	You **are** married.
		from Russia	They **are** from Russia.

Trinh Hong

33 years old
Single
Cambodia

Duong Bui

33 years old
Married
Vietnam

Alan Hart

64 years old
Divorced
United States

G   Write sentences about the people above.

EXAMPLE: (marital status) Duong __is married__ .

1. (marital status) Alan _____ .

2. (marital status) Trinh _____ and Alan _____ .

3. (age) Trinh and Duong _____ .

4. (age) Alan _____ .

(country) He _____ .

H   In a group, interview three students. Complete the chart.

What's your name?	Where are you from?	How old are you?	Are you married?

What does he look like?

GOAL ➤ **Describe people**

Vocabulary Grammar
Life Skills
Academic Pronunciation

5'11" = five feet, eleven inches
= five-eleven

A Look at Felipe's license. Complete the sentences.

1. Felipe's height is _____.

2. His weight is _____ pounds.

3. His hair is _____.

4. His eyes are _____.

5. He is _____ years old.

6. His address is _____ State Street.

His / Her

(Duong)
His hair is black.
His eyes are brown.

(Eva)
Her hair is white.
Her eyes are blue.

B Look at the licenses above. Complete the sentences about Duong and Eva.

1. Duong is _____. (height)

2. His _____. (weight)

3. His _____. (hair)

4. His _____. (eyes)

1. Eva is _____. (height)

2. Her _____. (weight)

3. Her _____. (hair)

4. Her _____. (eyes)

LESSON 2   **GOAL** ➤ Describe people

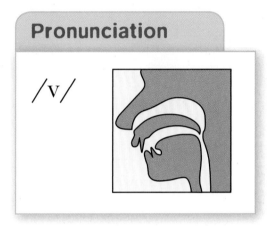
Vocabulary / Grammar / Life Skills / Academic / Pronunciation

C Study the chart with your classmates and teacher.

Simple Present: *Have*		
Subject	**Verb**	**Example sentence**
I, you, we, they	have	I **have** black hair. You **have** white hair.
he, she, it	has	He **has** brown eyes. She **has** blue eyes.

Pronunciation

/v/

CD 1
TR 15-18

D Listen and complete the chart.

Name	Height	Hair	Eyes	Age
1. Roberto	5'11"	black	brown	43
2. Trinh				
3. Gabriela				
4. Alan				

CD 1
TR 19

E Listen to the conversation.

A: What does <u>Roberto</u> look like?
B: <u>He</u> has <u>black hair</u> and <u>brown eyes</u>.
A: How tall is <u>he</u>?
B: <u>He</u> is <u>five feet, eleven inches</u> tall.
A: Thank you.

F Practice the conversation with information about Trinh, Gabriela, and Alan.

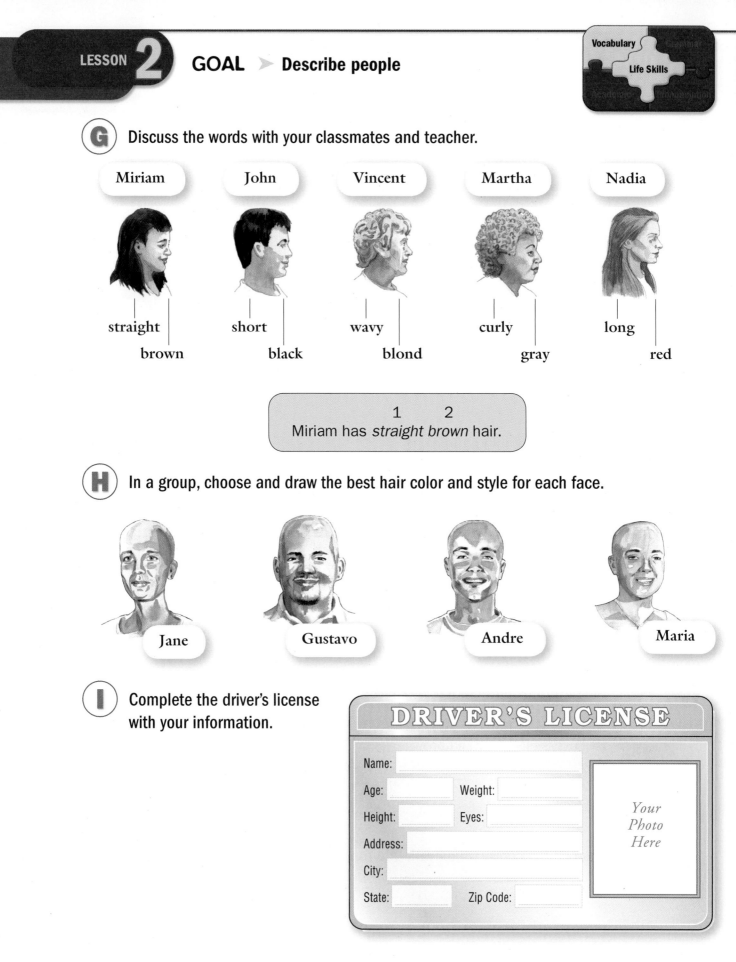

G Discuss the words with your classmates and teacher.

| Miriam | John | Vincent | Martha | Nadia |

straight | short | wavy | curly | long
brown | black | blond | gray | red

1   2
Miriam has *straight brown* hair.

H In a group, choose and draw the best hair color and style for each face.

Jane   Gustavo   Andre   Maria

I Complete the driver's license with your information.

DRIVER'S LICENSE

Name:
Age: Weight:
Height: Eyes:
Address:
City:
State: Zip Code:

Your Photo Here

Roberto's family

GOAL ➤ **Describe family relationships**

Who is in the picture?
What are they saying?

A **Listen to the conversation.**

CD 1
TR 20

Roberto: Duong, this is my mother, my father, and my sister.
Antonio: Nice to meet you, Duong. Where are you from?
Duong: I'm from Vietnam.
Antonio: Do your parents live here in the United States?
Duong: No. Right now they live in Vietnam.

B **Look at the people from the picture above. Write the words from the box under the pictures.**

friend	son	parents	sister	brother

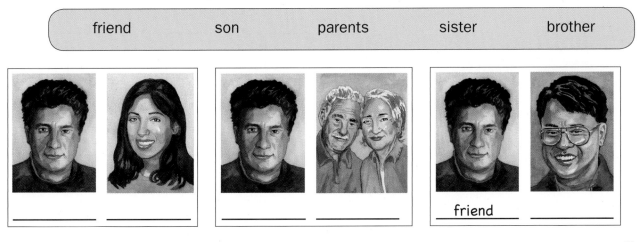

_____ _____   _____ _____   friend _____

GOAL ➤ **Describe family relationships**

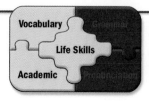

C Discuss the words with your classmates and teacher.

father	wife	children	grandson	uncle
mother	husband	grandfather	granddaughter	niece
brother	son	grandmother	aunt	nephew
sister	daughter			

D Look at the picture and write the names on the family tree. Then, listen to check your answers.

CD 1
TR 21

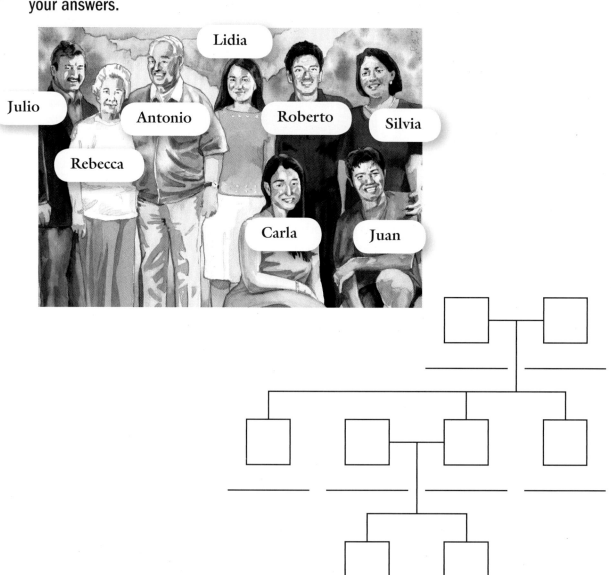

LESSON 3 **GOAL** ➤ **Describe family relationships**

E Practice the conversation.

Be verb
He **is** Roberto's brother.
They **are** Roberto's children.

Pronunciation

Prominence

➤ **WHO** is Silvia?

➤ **WHO** are Antonio and Rebecca?

Student A: Who is Silvia?
Student B: Silvia is Roberto's wife.

Student A: Who are Antonio and Rebecca?
Student B: They are Roberto's parents.

F Work with a partner. Ask questions about Roberto's family on page 8.

G Complete the family tree for your family.

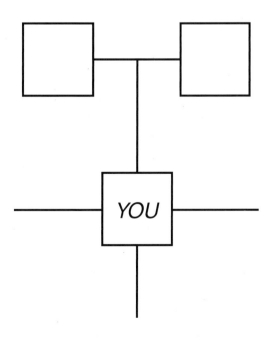

H Active Task. Find or draw a picture of your family and share it with the class.

I like sports and music.

GOAL ➤ Express preferences

Life Skills
Academic

CD 1
TR 22

A Listen. Put an *R* by things Roberto likes and an *S* by things Silvia likes.

movies ____R____

music _____

sports _____

games _____

computers _____

TV _____

books _____

restaurants _____

parks ____S____

B Complete the sentences.

1. Roberto likes _____movies_____.

2. Roberto likes _____.

3. Roberto likes _____.

4. Silvia likes _____.

5. Silvia likes _____.

6. Silvia likes _____.

7. They both like _____.

8. They both like _____.

GOAL ➤ Express preferences

 Study the chart with your classmates and teacher.

Simple Present: *Like*			
Subject	**Verb**	**Noun**	**Example sentence**
I, you, we, they	like	movies, music, sports, games, computers, TV, books, restaurants, parks	I **like** computers. They **like** books.
he, she, it	likes		He **likes** parks. She **likes** restaurants.

 Look at the diagram about Roberto's children.

Carla likes ...
restaurants
parks

Carla and Juan like ...
movies
music

Juan likes ...
sports
TV

E Discuss the diagram with a group.

F Complete the sentences with the correct form of *like*.

1. Antonio _____ computers.

2. Rebecca _____ parks.

3. Antonio and Rebecca _____ movies.

4. We _____ games.

5. The students _____ books.

6. I _____.

Pronunciation

Prominence

➤ What **THINGS** do you like?

G Talk to a partner and complete the diagram. Ask: *What things do you like?*

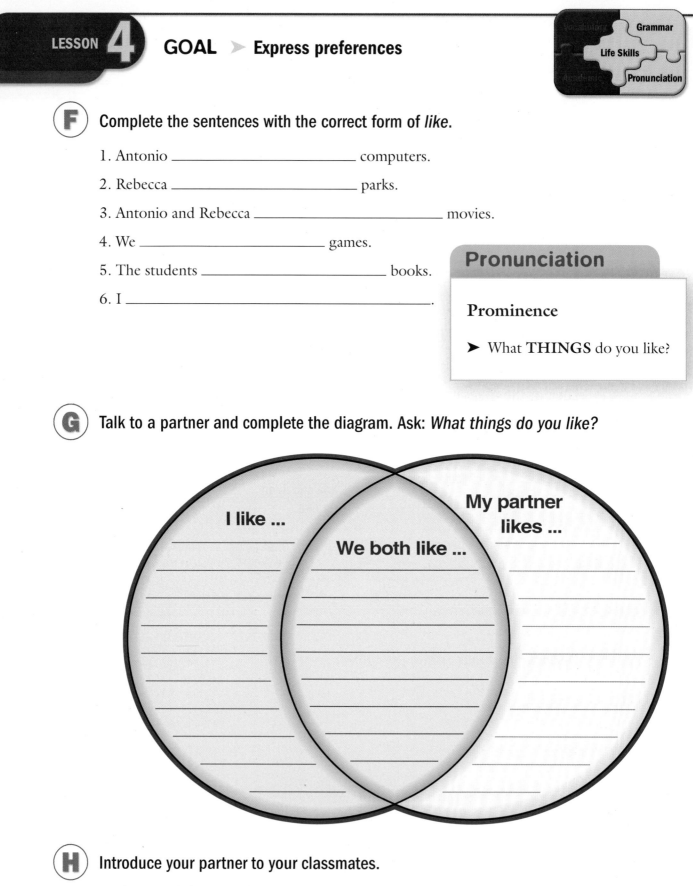

I like ...

We both like ...

My partner likes ...

H Introduce your partner to your classmates.

EXAMPLE: This is my friend Roberto. He is from Mexico. He is married and has two children. Roberto likes movies and books.

When do you study?

GOAL ➤ Plan a study schedule

A When does Roberto practice English? Look at the clocks, read the times, and write the information in the arrows.

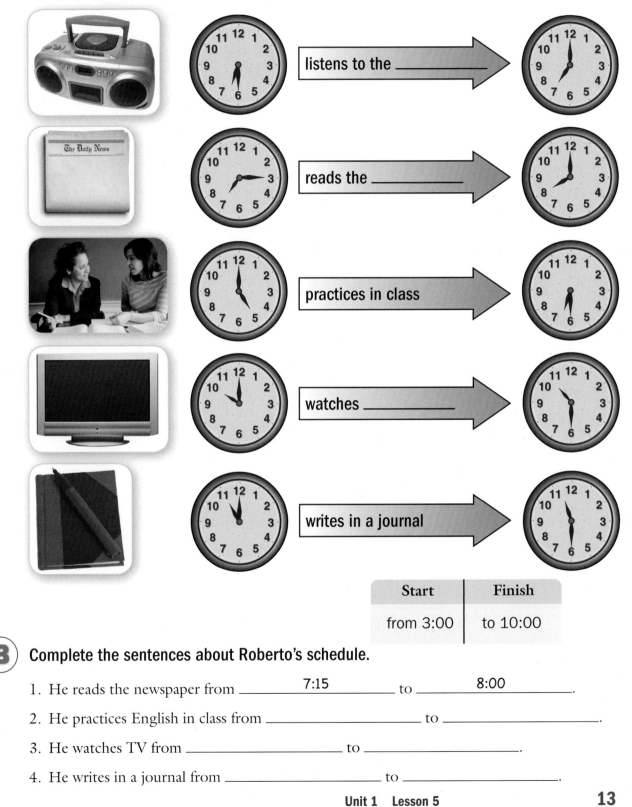

listens to the _____

reads the _____

practices in class

watches _____

writes in a journal

Start	Finish
from 3:00	to 10:00

B Complete the sentences about Roberto's schedule.

1. He reads the newspaper from _____7:15_____ to _____8:00_____.

2. He practices English in class from _____ to _____.

3. He watches TV from _____ to _____.

4. He writes in a journal from _____ to _____.

LESSON 5 **GOAL** > **Plan a study schedule**

Life Skills
Academic

C Look at the clocks. Write the times.

1. Lidia reads the newspaper at ___6:45___.

2. Lidia listens to the radio at _____.

3. Lidia practices English in class at _____.

4. Lidia writes in a journal at _____.

D Write Lidia's schedule.

Time	Activity
6:45	reads the newspaper

E Listen and write Juan's schedule.

CD 1
TR 23

Start time	End time	Activity
6:00	6:30	eats breakfast
		reads the newspaper
		listens to the radio
		writes in a journal
		practices English in class

F Write sentences about Juan's schedule.

1. Juan ___eats breakfast___ from ___6:00___ to ___6:30___.

2. Juan _____ from _____ to _____.

3. Juan _____ from _____ to _____.

4. Juan _____ from _____ to _____.

5. Juan _____ from _____ to _____.

 When do you practice English? Complete the chart.

	From	To	Activity
in the morning			
in the afternoon			
at night			

 Talk to a partner. Ask: *When do you practice English?* Complete the chart.

	From	To	Activity
in the morning			
in the afternoon			
at night			

I Report the information about your partner to a group.

Review

A Complete the chart about Trinh, Duong, and Alan. (Lesson 1)

Trinh Hong

Alan Hart

33 years old
Single
Cambodia

33 years old
Married
Vietnam

64 years old
Divorced
United States

Name	Marital status	Age	Country
1. Trinh Hong			
2. Duong Bui			
3. Alan Hart			

B Bubble in the correct answer. (Lessons 1 and 2)

EXAMPLE: My name _____ Duong.   ○ am   ● is   ○ was

1. I _____ from Vietnam.

  ○ am   ○ is   ○ are

2. Roberto _____ from Mexico.

  ○ am   ○ is   ○ are

3. Roberto and Duong _____ students.

  ○ am   ○ is   ○ are

4. Roberto and Duong _____ black hair.

  ○ has   ○ have   ○ are

5. Roberto _____ one brother.

  ○ has   ○ have   ○ is

6. Silvia _____ 23 years old.

  ○ has   ○ have   ○ is

C Read the sentences and complete Duong's license. (Lesson 2)

Duong's birth date is July 2, 1979.
His address is 23 South Street.
He lives in New York City, NY.
He is 5'6'' tall.
He has brown eyes.
His zip code is 10038.
His weight is 165 pounds.

DRIVER'S LICENSE

Name:
Age: Weight:
Height: Eyes:
Address:
City:
State: Zip Code:

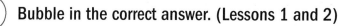

D Match the questions and answers. Write the correct letter next to each number. (Lesson 2)

1. __d__ What's your name?   a. 6 feet, 2 inches.

2. _____ Where are you from?   b. 28.

3. _____ How old are you?   c. Yes, I am.

4. _____ What is your weight?   d. Ernesto Gonzalez.

5. _____ What is your height?   e. 195 pounds.

6. _____ Are you married?   f. Colombia.

E What is the relationship? Look at page 8 and fill in the missing words. (Lesson 3)

1. Silvia is Juan's mother, and Juan is Silvia's _____ son _____.

2. Juan is Carla's brother, and Carla is Juan's _____.

3. Roberto is Carla's father, and Carla is Roberto's _____.

4. Roberto and Silvia are Juan and Carla's _____.

5. Juan and Carla are Roberto and Silvia's _____.

F Unscramble the family words. (Lesson 3)

1. tehrfa   _____ father _____

2. nos   _____

3. dlehcinr   _____

4. htreaudg   _____

5. tehrmo   _____

Review

G What does Silvia like? Fill in the missing words. (Lesson 4)

 1. She likes _____TV_____.

 3. She likes the _____.

 2. She likes _____.

 4. She likes the _____.

H How does Roberto practice English? Fill in the missing verbs. (Lesson 5)

 1. He ___listens___ to the radio.

 3. He _____ the newspaper.

 2. He _____ TV.

 4. He _____ in his journal.

I What time is it? Write the times. (Lesson 5)

1. It's ___11:30___. 2. It's _____. 3. It's _____. 4. It's _____.

J Describe two of your classmates. (Lesson 2)

EXAMPLE: ___John has short black hair and brown eyes.___

_____

_____

My Dictionary

Make flash cards to improve your vocabulary.

1. Choose four new words from this unit.

2. Write each word on an index card or on a sheet of paper.

3. On the back of the index card or paper, draw a picture, find and write a sentence from the book with the word, and write the page number.

4. Study the words.

Are you <u>married</u>?
page 2

Learner Log

Circle how well you learned each item and write the page number where you learned it.

1. I can give personal information.
   EXAMPLE: age, marital status, and country

   Yes   Maybe   No   Page _____

2. I can describe people.
   EXAMPLE: hair, eyes, height, and weight

   Yes   Maybe   No   Page _____

3. I can describe my family.
   EXAMPLE: brother, sister, parents

   Yes   Maybe   No   Page _____

4. I can express preferences.
   EXAMPLE: *I like books.*

   Yes   Maybe   No   Page _____

5. I can make a study schedule.
   EXAMPLE: *I read from 3:00 to 4:00.*

   Yes   Maybe   No   Page _____

Rank what you like to do best from 1 to 6. 1 is your favorite activity. Your teacher will help you.

_____ Practice listening

_____ Practice speaking

_____ Practice reading

_____ Practice writing

_____ Learn new words

_____ Learn grammar

In the next unit, I want to practice more

_____.

Team Project

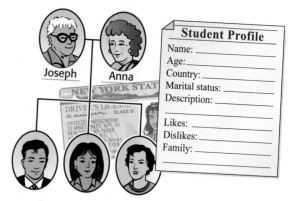

Create a student profile.

In this project, you will work together to create a student profile for one person on your team.

1. Form a team with four or five students. In your team, you need:

POSITION	JOB	STUDENT NAME
Student 1: **Team Leader**	See that everyone speaks English. See that everyone participates.	
Student 2: **Secretary**	Complete the student profile with help from the team.	
Student 3: **Student for profile**	Give personal information for introductions.	
Students 4/5: **Hosts or Hostesses**	Introduce student to other groups.	

2. Create a student profile sheet. Write questions. See page 17 for help.

3. Choose one student in your group to create a profile for.

4. Complete the student profile sheet by asking questions. Each student in the group asks three or more questions.

5. Practice introducing and describing the student to other groups. Use the profile sheet.

6. Create more student profiles if you have time.

Let's go shopping!

GOALS

➤ Identify places to make purchases

➤ Make purchases

➤ Identify articles of clothing

➤ Describe clothing

➤ Describe items in a store

LESSON 1

Shopping

GOAL ➤ Identify places to make purchases

A Read about Van.

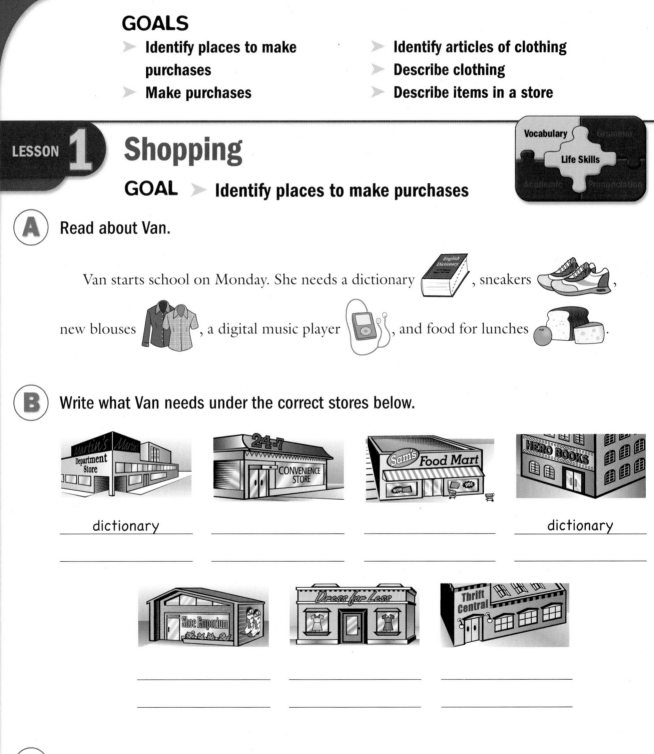

Van starts school on Monday. She needs a dictionary, sneakers, new blouses, a digital music player, and food for lunches.

B Write what Van needs under the correct stores below.

dictionary   dictionary

C What other things can you buy at each store? Make a list with a group.

GOAL ➤ **Identify places to make purchases**

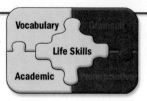

 D Listen to Van and her husband. Circle the best place to get each item.

CD 1
TR 24

Product	Type of store	
1. a radio	(a department store)	a convenience store
2. shoes	a shoe store	a department store
3. shirts	a clothing store	a department store
4. a dictionary	a bookstore	a department store
5. bread, cheese, and fruit	a supermarket	a convenience store

Pronunciation

Stress and Rhythm
↓
➤ WHERE do VAN // and her HÜSband // SHOP for a RÄDio?
➤ At a dePARTment store.

E Practice pronouncing the sentences with a partner.

1. Van // shops at the department store // every Wednesday.

2. Her husband // likes to buy food // at the supermarket.

3. Where's // the convenience store?

4. The bookstore // has dictionaries.

F Use the information in Exercise D to practice the conversation. Use *shoes, shirts, a dictionary,* and *bread, cheese,* and *fruit* in new conversations.

Student A: Where do Van and her husband shop for a radio?
Student B: at a department store

 Study the chart with your classmates and teacher.

Simple Present: *Shop*		
Subject	**Verb**	**Example sentence**
I, you, we, they	shop	I **shop** for shoes at a department store. You **shop** for bread at a convenience store. We **shop** for food at a supermarket. They **shop** for books at a bookstore.
he, she, it	shops	He **shops** for shoes at a shoe store. She **shops** for dresses at a clothing store.

H Complete the sentences with the correct form of *shop*.

EXAMPLE: Van _____shops_____ for a radio at a department store.

1. They _____ for food at a supermarket.

2. We _____ for sneakers at a shoe store.

3. He _____ for soda at a convenience store.

4. I _____ for a dictionary at a bookstore.

I Make a bar graph. How many of your classmates shop in different types of stores?

EXAMPLE:

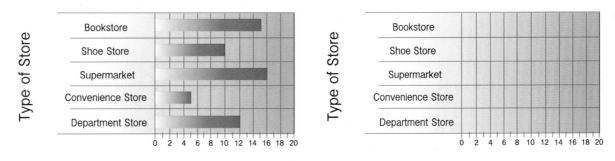

Number of Students   Number of Students

 J **Active Task.** Go to a mall or use the Internet. Find the name of three clothing stores that you like. Report them to the class.

Van's purchases

GOAL ➤ Make purchases

Life Skills
Academic

A Look at the receipts. What are the totals? What is the tax?

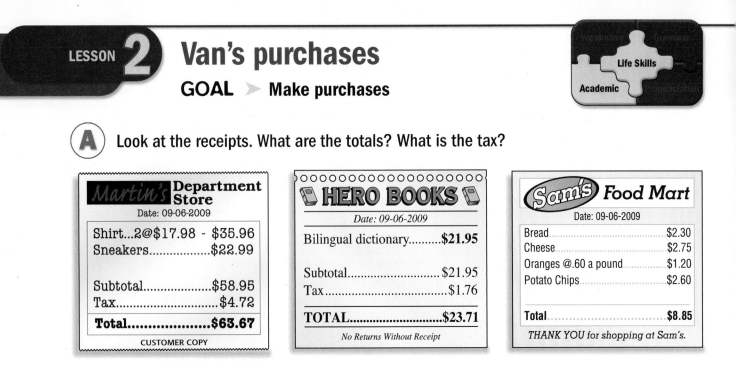

Martin's Department Store
Date: 09-06-2009

Shirt...2@$17.98 -	$35.96
Sneakers...............	$22.99
Subtotal................	$58.95
Tax.........................	$4.72
Total....................	**$63.67**

CUSTOMER COPY

HERO BOOKS
Date: 09-06-2009

Bilingual dictionary........	**$21.95**
Subtotal......................	$21.95
Tax..............................	$1.76
TOTAL..........................	**$23.71**

No Returns Without Receipt

Sam's Food Mart
Date: 09-06-2009

Bread..............................	$2.30
Cheese............................	$2.75
Oranges @.60 a pound............	$1.20
Potato Chips.....................	$2.60
Total............................	**$8.85**

THANK YOU for shopping at Sam's.

B How much is the total for the shirts, sneakers, bilingual dictionary, and food?

$63.67 (clothes) + $23.71 (dictionary) + $8.85 (food) = _____

C Listen and circle the amounts you hear.

CD 1
TR 25

EXAMPLE:	$12.50	$2.15	($22.50)	$22.15
1. $12.95	$34.15	$34.50	$45.50	
2. $13.00	$30.00	$33.00	$43.00	
3. $ .57	$57.00	$15.70	$17.00	
4. $19.75	$17.90	$79.00	$77.95	

D Listen and write the prices.

CD 1
TR 26

LANG'S DEPARTMENT STORE

vacuum	washing machine	candy bar	paper	telephone
1. $ 98.99	2. $	3. $	4. $	5. $

GOAL ➤ **Make purchases**

Vocabulary
Life Skills

E Practice asking about prices. Look at Exercise D on page 24 for information.

EXAMPLE:
Student A: Excuse me, how much is the <u>vacuum</u>?
Student B: $98.99.
Student A: Thank you.

Be verb
How much *is* the vacuum?
How much *are* the candy bars?

F Write the words from the box under the pictures.

a nickel	a ten-dollar bill	a penny	a one-dollar bill
a twenty-dollar bill	a quarter	a five-dollar bill	a dime

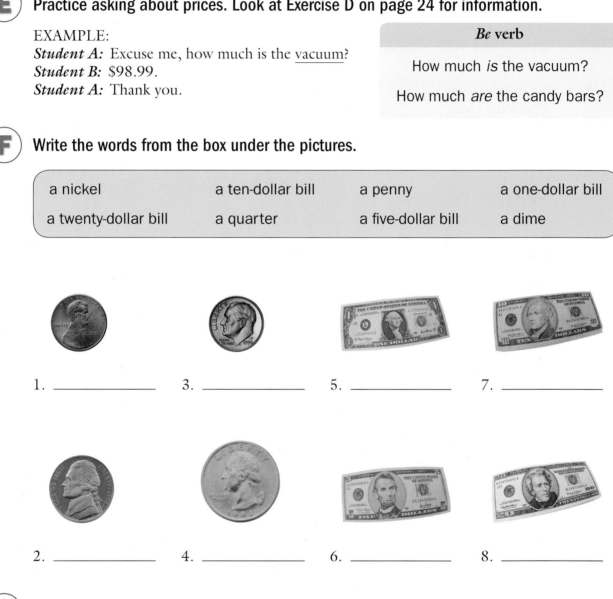

1. _____   3. _____   5. _____   7. _____

2. _____   4. _____   6. _____   8. _____

G What bills and coins do you need for these items? Tell a partner.

LANG'S DEPARTMENT STORE

$53.99 $75.50 $23.71   DICTIONARY

H Read the check.

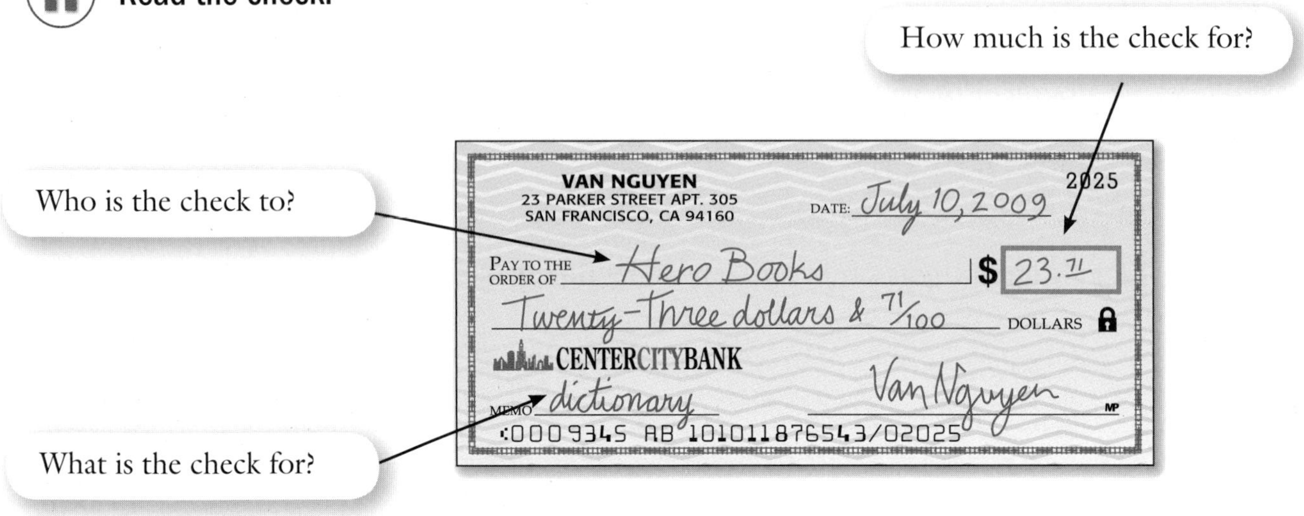

How much is the check for?

Who is the check to?

VAN NGUYEN
23 PARKER STREET APT. 305
SAN FRANCISCO, CA 94160

DATE: *July 10, 2009*   2025

PAY TO THE
ORDER OF *Hero Books*   **$** *23.71*

Twenty-Three dollars & 71/100   DOLLARS 🔒

CENTERCITYBANK

MEMO *dictionary*   *Van Nguyen*   MP

⑆0009345 AB 10101l876543/02025

What is the check for?

I Look at the items in Exercises D and G. Which items do you want to buy?
Write a check for one of the items.

_____   2026

_____   DATE:_____

_____

PAY TO THE
ORDER OF_____   **$** [   ]

_____   DOLLARS 🔒

CENTERCITYBANK

MEMO_____   _____   MP

⑆0009345 AB 10101l876543/02026

J **Active Task.** Visit some banks or use the Internet. Find the names of three banks
where you can open a checking account.

Buying new clothes

GOAL ➤ **Identify articles of clothing**

CD 1
TR 27

A Write the correct letter under each type of clothing. Then, listen for the missing prices.

a. suit

b. t-shirt

c. ties

d. hat

e. sweater

f. dress

g. socks

h. baseball cap

i. sneakers

j. blouse

k. coat

l. skirt

B Work in a group. Write the clothing words from Exercise A in the chart. Add other clothing words that you know.

Women's	Men's	Both

C Study the charts with your classmates and teacher.

Be Verb (Questions)			
Question words	Be	Singular or plural noun	Example question
how much (money)	is	the dress the suit	How much **is** the dress? How much **is** the suit?
how much (money)	are	the socks the ties	How much **are** the socks? How much **are** the ties?

Be Verb (Answers)		
Singular or plural noun or pronoun	Be	Example answer
it	is	It **is** $48. It**'s** $48. (The dress **is** $48.) It **is** $285. It**'s** $285. (The suit **is** $285.)
they	are	They **are** $12. They**'re** $12. (The socks **are** $12.) They **are** $22. They**'re** $22. (The ties **are** $22.)

D Practice the conversation.

Student A: How much is the dress?
Student B: It's $48.

E Ask a partner about the prices. Use the conversation in Exercise D.

Student A asks Student B: Student B asks Student A:

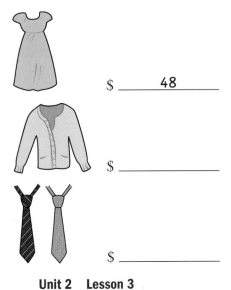

$ _____ 48 _____

$ _____

$ _____

$ _____

$ _____

$ _____

 Read about Gabriela.

Gabriela needs a new shirt, a skirt, and a hat. She shops at Dress for Less. It is a good store. She has $75.

 Look at the ad on page 27 for prices. Circle *Yes* or *No*.

1. Gabriela shops at Lang's department store.	Yes	No
2. Gabriela has $75.	Yes	No
3. Gabriela can buy a shirt, a skirt, and a hat.	Yes	No

 Look at the ad on page 27. You have $75. What different items can you buy? Write the items and their prices. Then, talk in a group.

_____   _____   _____

_____   _____   _____

I **Active Task.** Find a clothing ad in a newspaper. What can you buy for $100?

What color is your shirt?

GOAL ➤ **Describe clothing**

Vocabulary · Grammar
Life Skills
Academic · Pronunciation

A Listen and point to the clothing you hear about in the conversation.

CD 1
TR 28

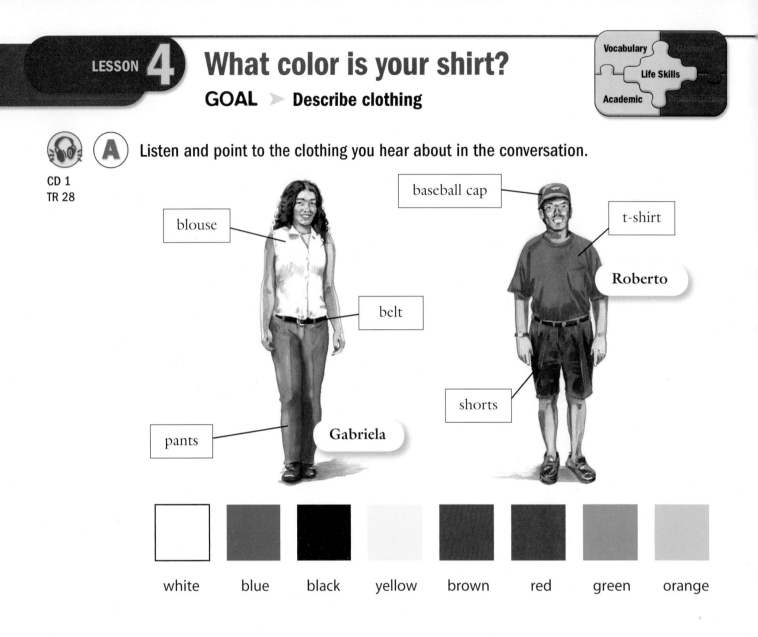

baseball cap

blouse

t-shirt

Roberto

belt

shorts

pants

Gabriela

white   blue   black   yellow   brown   red   green   orange

B Complete the chart with the words from the picture. Then, add more clothing words.

Singular	Plural		Plural only
t-shirt	t-shirts		

 C Study the chart with your classmates and teacher. Use the words from the box to complete the chart.

his	her
my	our
your	their

Pronoun	Possessive Adjectives
I	_____My_____ shirt is blue. _____ shoes are black.
you	_____ baseball cap is blue. _____ shorts are brown.
he	_____ belt is black. _____ sandals are brown.
she	_____ blouse is pink. _____ shoes are white.
we	_____ shirts are white. _____ pants are blue.
they	_____ dresses are red. _____ shoes are black.

D Look at page 30. Answer the questions.

EXAMPLE: What color are Roberto's shorts?

_____His shorts are brown._____

1. What color is Gabriela's blouse?

   _____

2. What color are Gabriela and Roberto's belts?

   _____

3. What color are Gabriela's pants?

   _____

4. What color is Roberto's t-shirt?

   _____

5. What color are Gabriela and Roberto's shoes?

   _____

GOAL ➤ **Describe clothing**

E Talk to a partner and describe your classmates' clothes. Then, write sentences.

My	**His**
My shirt is _____ .	His shirt is _____ .
My pants are _____ .	_____
My _____ .	_____
_____	_____
_____	_____

Your	**Her**
Your shirt is _____ .	Her shirt is _____ .
_____	_____
_____	_____
_____	_____
_____	_____

Our	**Their**
Our shirts are _____ .	Their _____ .
_____	_____
_____	_____
_____	_____
_____	_____

F With a different partner, describe your classmates by their clothes. Let your partner guess who the classmates are.

EXAMPLE: *Student A:* Her blouse is blue.
Student B: Amy?

G Look around the classroom. In groups, make a list of clothes by color.

Red	Blue	Green	Orange
Carolina's sweater			

A large TV or a small TV?

GOAL ➤ Describe items in a store

Vocabulary
Life Skills

A Look at the pictures. Write a word under each picture.

1. Do you want a small CD player or a large CD player?

small   large

2. Do you want a new house or an old house?

_____   _____

3. Do you want a new car or a used car?

_____   _____

4. Do you want a striped shirt or a checked shirt?

_____   _____

5. Do you want a large blouse or a medium blouse?

L   M

_____   _____

6. Do you want small pants or medium pants?

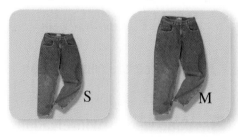

S   M

_____   _____

B Complete the chart. Write the new words from Exercise A.

Size	Age	Pattern
large	used	striped

Where is Tatsuya?
What does he want?

C Listen to the conversation with your books closed. What does Tatsuya want to buy?

CD 1
TR 29

Tatsuya: Excuse me. I want a TV.
Salesperson: A big TV or a small TV?
Tatsuya: I want a small TV.
Salesperson: OK, how about this one?
Tatsuya: Yes, that's good. How much is it?
Salesperson: It's $135.
Tatsuya: I'll take it!

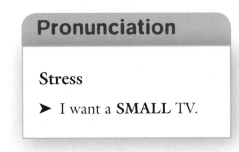
Pronunciation

Stress

➤ I want a **SMALL** TV.

D Practice the conversation with a partner.

E Practice new conversations. Use the information below. Use the conversation in Exercise C as an example.

Student A is the customer. Student B is the salesperson.			Student B is the customer. Student A is the salesperson.		
1. blouse:	medium/small	$24	1. car:	used/new	$12,000
2. CD player:	large/small	$34	2. house:	old/new	$300,000
3. refrigerator:	new/used	$210	3. sweater:	striped/checked	$42
4. shirt:	small/medium	$18	4. dress:	large/medium	$33

LESSON **5**

GOAL ➤ Describe items in a store

> Grammar
> Life Skills
> Academic

F Study the chart with your classmates and teacher.

Simple Present: *Want*		
Subject	**Verb**	**Example sentence**
I, you, we, they	want	I **want** a large TV.
he, she, it	wants	He **wants** a new house.

CD 1
TR 30–33

G Listen to the conversations and circle the correct answers.

1.

a small TV · · · a large TV · · · a new TV

2.

a new house · · · an old house · · · a small house

3.

a small blouse · · · a medium blouse · · · a large blouse

4.

a new car · · · an old car · · · a used car

H Complete the sentences with the correct form of *want*. Use the information from Exercise G.

1. Tatsuya _____ a small TV.

2. Emily and Steve _____ .

3. Gabriela _____ .

4. Ivan and Natasha _____ .

I With a partner, write a conversation like the ones you heard in Exercise G. Present it to the class.

Review

 A Listen and write the prices in Column 1. (Lesson 2)

Item	How much is it?	Where can you buy it?	Describe it.
		department store	black and white
	$456.78		

 B Complete columns 2 and 3 in the chart above with your ideas.
(Lessons 1, 2, and 5)

C Look at the receipts. What is the total of all three receipts? (Lesson 2)

MARTIN'S Department Store
Date: 09-26-2009

Shirt	2@$27.98
Tax	$ 4.48
Total	$60.44

ELECTRONICS SURPLUS
Date: 09-26-2009

Magi big screen TV

	$789.55
Tax	$ 63.16
Total	$852.71

Shoe Emporium
Date: 09-26-2009

Black Loafers	$44.95
Tax	$ 3.60
Total	$48.55

___

 D Write a check for the first receipt. (Lesson 2)

2026

DATE:_____

PAY TO THE ORDER OF _____ $ [   ]

_____ DOLLARS 🔒

CENTERCITYBANK

MEMO_____   MP

⑆000934⑆ AB 10101187654 3/02026

E Write the word under each picture. (Lesson 3)

1. _____   2. _____   3. _____

Review

Eva

Duong

F Describe the pictures. Use *his, her,* or *their*. (Lesson 4)

1. What color is Eva's hat? _Her hat is blue._

2. What color is Duong's cap? _____

3. What color is Duong's shirt? _____

4. What color are Eva's pants? _____

5. What color are Eva and Duong's shoes? _____

6. What color is Duong's belt? _____

G Write sentences about things you want in Unit 2. (Lessons 1–5)

EXAMPLE: _I want a vacuum._

1. _____

2. _____

3. _____

4. _____

H Talk to a partner. Write sentences about things your partner wants in Unit 2. (Lessons 1–5)

EXAMPLE: _Eduardo wants a car._

1. _____

2. _____

3. _____

4. _____

My Dictionary

Make flash cards to improve your vocabulary.

1. Choose four new words from this unit.

2. Write each word on an index card or on a sheet of paper.

3. On the back of the index card or paper, draw a picture, find and write a sentence from the book with the word, and write the page number.

4. Study the words.

Her blouse is <u>blue.</u>

page 32

Learner Log

Circle how well you learned each item and write the page number where you learned it.

1. I can name different kinds of stores.
   EXAMPLE: department stores, bookstores

   Yes   Maybe   No   Page _____

2. I can read receipts and write checks.

   Yes   Maybe   No   Page _____

3. I can identify clothing.
   EXAMPLE: blouse, dress, skirt

   Yes   Maybe   No   Page _____

4. I can describe clothing.
   EXAMPLE: blue shirt, red pants

   Yes   Maybe   No   Page _____

5. I can describe other items.
   EXAMPLE: small TV or large TV

   Yes   Maybe   No   Page _____

Rank what you like to do best from 1 to 6. 1 is your favorite activity. Your teacher will help you.

_____ Practice listening

_____ Practice speaking

_____ Practice reading

_____ Practice writing

_____ Learn new words

_____ Learn grammar

In the next unit, I want to practice more

_____ .

Team Project

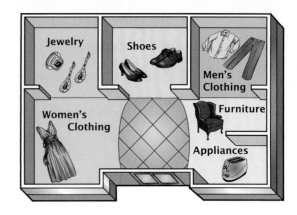

Plan a department store.

In this project, you will plan a department store and present it to the class.

1. Form a team with four or five students. In your team, you need:

POSITION	JOB	STUDENT NAME
Student 1: **Team Leader**	See that everyone speaks English. See that everyone participates.	
Student 2: **Architect**	With help from the team, draw the floor plan.	
Student 3: **Sales Manager**	With help from the team, list the prices of the items in your store.	
Students 4/5: **Writers**	With help from the team, prepare a role-play to present to the class.	

2. Choose a name for your department store.

3. Draw a floor plan of your store.

4. Make a list of ten things you sell. Include their prices. Where are the items located on your floor plan?

5. Prepare a role-play in which a person in your group talks to a salesperson and buys some things. You can also make checks and receipts. Students in your group can take on the roles of a salesperson, a cashier, a customer or customers, and a manager.

6. Practice the role-play and present it to the class.

Food

GOALS

➤ Identify common meals and foods

➤ Interpret food advertisements

➤ Express needs

➤ Compare prices

➤ Place orders

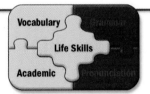

LESSON **1**

What's for lunch?

GOAL ➤ Identify common meals and foods

A Read about Dave.

I'm Dave Chen. I'm an English teacher in Florida. I like to eat! I eat a big breakfast in the morning, a small lunch at noon, and a big dinner around six o'clock.

Where is Dave?
Predict what food he will eat.

B Look at the picture above. Write the foods you see in the chart.

Breakfast (Morning)	Lunch (Afternoon)	Dinner (Evening)
	pizza	

GOAL ➤ **Identify common meals and foods**

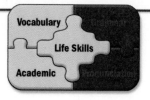

Vocabulary

Life Skills

Academic

C Read the foods in the box with your classmates and teacher.

a hamburger	spaghetti	toast	french fries	cereal
a sandwich	roast beef	eggs	fried chicken	

D What do you think Dave eats for breakfast, lunch, and dinner? Complete the diagram with the foods from the box.

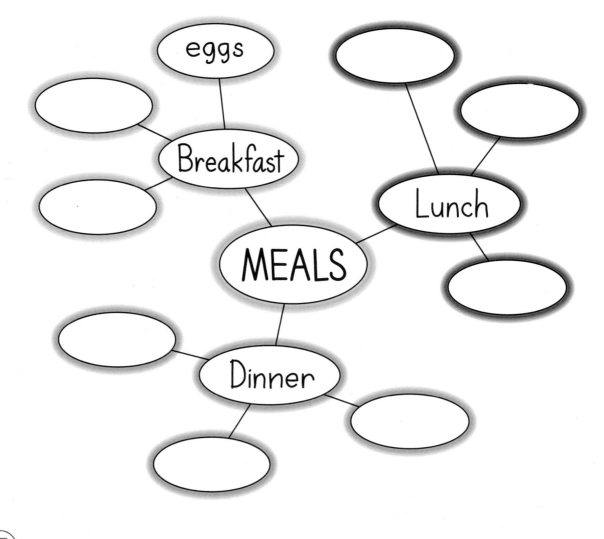

E Listen to Dave and check the information in Exercise D.

CD 1
TR 35

GOAL ➤ **Identify common meals and foods**

 Practice the conversation.

Mario: What do you like for lunch?
Jim: I like egg rolls. How about you?
Mario: I like tacos.

G **Practice in groups of four or five.**

Student A: What do you like for lunch?
Student B: I like hamburgers.
Student C: He likes hamburgers and I like sandwiches.
Student D: He likes hamburgers, she likes sandwiches, and I like soup.

Simple Present
I like . . .
He/She likes . . .

H **What do you eat for breakfast, lunch, and dinner?**

Breakfast	Lunch	Dinner

I **Write sentences about what you like for breakfast, lunch, and dinner.**

1. I like _____ for breakfast.

2. _____ for lunch.

3. _____.

It's in the newspaper.

GOAL ➤ Interpret food advertisements

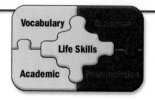

A Read the advertisement with your classmates and teacher.

 B Listen to Duong and his wife, Minh, make a shopping list. What do they need to buy? Write *Yes* or *No*.

CD 1
TR 36

Do they need . . .	Yes/No
ground beef?	Yes
spaghetti?	
milk?	
carrots?	
tomatoes?	
peanut butter?	
soda?	
avocados?	

C Write sentences about what Duong and Minh buy.

1. They buy ground beef.

2. _____

3. _____

GOAL ➤ **Interpret food advertisements**

D Study the advertisement with your classmates and teacher.

E Complete the chart with the information in Exercise D.

Product	Container or Quantity (*jar, box, bag, pound, package, gallon, each, or loaf*)	Price
cookies		$2.75
	bag	$2.75
		$.99
	each	
	each	
	each	$1.25
	each	$.68
		$3.25
	jar	$1.89
peanut butter		
	loaf	
	package	$1.25
		$1.00
tomatoes		
	pound	
	pound	$2.25

Be Verb	
How much **is the**	bread? peanut butter?
How much **are the**	tomatoes? potato chips?

 Practice the conversation. Student A asks questions. Student B looks at the advertisement on page 45 to answer. Ask about *peanut butter, tomatoes, milk,* and *cookies*.

Student A: How much is the peanut butter?
Student B: It's $3.25 a jar.

Student A: How much are the tomatoes?
Student B: They are $.68 a pound.

G **Practice the conversation. Student B asks questions. Student A looks at the advertisement on page 45 to answer. Ask about *bread, potato chips, soda,* and *apples*.**

Student A: How much is the bread?
Student B: It's $1.98 a loaf.

Student A: How much are the potato chips?
Student B: They are $2.75 a bag.

H In a group, make your own food advertisement.

NewsObserver   Sunday, October

I **Active Task. Look at a food advertisement in a local newspaper. Are the prices in your advertisement in Exercise H more expensive or cheaper?**

What do we need?

GOAL ➤ Express needs

Where is Duong?
What is Duong eating?

A Read Duong's story.

My name is Duong. I'm from Vietnam. I study at North Creek Adult School. It is very expensive to eat out every day, so I bring my lunch to school. My wife and I go to the store every Saturday. We buy bread and meat for my sandwiches.

B Answer the questions. Bubble in *True* or *False*.

	True	False
1. Duong buys his lunch at school.	○	○
2. Duong and his son go to the store every Saturday.	○	○
3. Duong and his wife buy bread and meat for sandwiches.	○	○

CD 1
TR 37

C Listen to the conversation between Duong and Minh. What do they need at the supermarket? Check (✔) the foods.

SHOPPING LIST
_____ ham
_____ tuna fish
_____ peanut butter
_____ jelly
_____ turkey
_____ chicken
_____ salami

GOAL ➤ **Express needs**

D Study the words for food containers. Write the correct word under each picture.

bag   bottle   ~~can~~   jar   box   package

1. a ____can____   3. a _____   5. a _____
   of soup   of water   of cheese

2. a _____   4. a _____   6. a _____
   of cookies   of mustard   of potato chips

E What other foods go into each container?

Container	Food
can/cans	beans, coffee
bottle/bottles	
package/packages	
box/boxes	
jar/jars	
bag/bags	

Pronunciation

Plurals

/z/	/iz/
jar*z*	packag*iz*
bag*z*	box*iz*
can*z*	

F Complete the sentences by adding words from Exercise E.

1. Duong needs three cans of ____coffee_____ .

2. He needs four bottles of _____ .

3. He needs two packages of _____ .

4. _____ three boxes of _____ .

5. _____

6. _____

LESSON 3 **GOAL** ➤ Express needs

 Study the chart with your classmates and teacher.

Simple Present		
Subject	**Verb**	**Example sentence**
I, you, we, they	eat like need want make	I **eat** tacos for lunch. You **like** eggs for breakfast. We **need** three cans of corn. They **want** three boxes of cookies. I **make** sandwiches for lunch.
he, she, it	eats likes needs wants makes	He **eats** pizza for dinner. She **likes** tomato soup. He **needs** three pounds of tomatoes. She **wants** two bottles of water. She **makes** sandwiches for Duong.

H **Read the shopping list.**

SHOPPING LIST

6 bottles of water
3 cans of soup
1 jar of jelly
3 packages of cheese

I **Complete the sentences with the correct form of the verbs in parentheses. Fill in the correct containers for the food items.**

1. Duong ____needs____ (need) one ____jar____ of jelly.
2. They _____ (like) soup at night.
3. Duong _____ (eat) sandwiches at school.
4. Minh _____ (make) sandwiches for Duong.
5. They _____ (want) three _____ of cheese.

 Make a list of things you need at the store. Tell your partner what you need.

Unit 3   Lesson 3   **49**

LESSON 4   What's cheaper?

GOAL ➤ Compare prices

Life Skills
Academic

A   Look at Duong's shopping list. Look at the advertisement on page 44 for Puente Market and the advertisement on page 45 for Food City. Which store is cheaper for Duong?

> SHOPPING LIST
>
> 2 pounds of ground beef
>
> 3 pounds of tomatoes
>
> avocados
>
> carrots

B   Study the graph. Fill in the missing information.

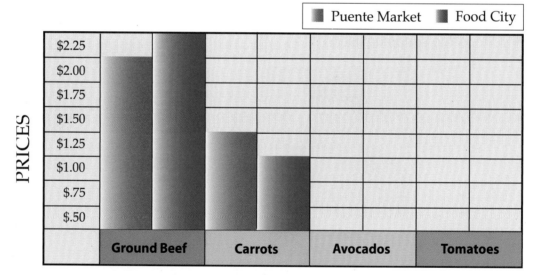

C   Complete the chart and calculate the totals.

	Puente Market	Food City
Ground beef	$1.99	$2.25
Carrots		
Avocados		
Tomatoes		
Total		

GOAL ➤ **Compare prices**

D Study the charts with your classmates and teacher.

Cheaper		
	Question	**Answer**
Singular	Where is ground beef cheaper?	It's **cheaper** at Puente Market.
Plural	Where are carrots cheaper?	They're **cheaper** at Food City.

More expensive		
	Question	**Answer**
Singular	Where is ground beef more expensive?	It's **more expensive** at Food City.
Plural	Where are carrots more expensive?	They're **more expensive** at Puente Market.

Pronunciation

Rhythm
➤ WHERE is ground **beef cheaper?**
➤ WHERE is ground **beef** more **expensive?**

➤ WHERE are **carrots cheaper?**
➤ WHERE are **carrots** more **expensive?**

E Use the information on page 50. Practice comparing prices.

EXAMPLE: *Student A:* I need some ground beef. Where is it cheaper?
　　　　　 Student B: It's cheaper at Puente Market.

F Use the information on page 50. Practice comparing prices.

EXAMPLE: *Student A:* I buy ground beef at Puente Market.
　　　　　 Student B: Why?
　　　　　 Student A: It's more expensive at Food City.

Life Skills
Academic

G Read the paragraph about Sebastien.

I shop at Food City. I like the bananas and oranges there. The fruit is more expensive, but I like the store. They have good specials, too. Food City is near my home.

H Answer the questions. Bubble in *True* or *False*.

	True	False
1. Sebastien shops at Puente Market.	○	○
2. The fruit at Puente Market is cheaper.	○	○
3. Food City has bananas and oranges.	○	○

CD 1
TR 38

I Listen to Sebastien ask about prices. Complete the charts.

Puente Market	
Fruit	**Price**
bananas	$.92
oranges	
pears	
apples	

Food City	
Fruit	**Price**
bananas	$.98
oranges	
pears	
apples	

J Complete the bar graph about the two markets. Use the information from Exercise I.

	Puente Market	Food City	Puente Market	Food City	Puente Market	Food City	Puente Market	Food City
$2.50								
$2.00								
$1.75								
$1.50								
$1.25								
$1.00								
$ .75								
	bananas		oranges		pears		apples	

K What store do you shop at? Why? Tell a group.

 L **Active Task.** As a class, choose one food item. Choose two stores in your neighborhood or go to the Internet. Compare prices of the food item. Which store is cheaper?

LESSON 5

Buying lunch

GOAL ➤ Place orders

Vocabulary · Grammar · Life Skills · Pronunciation

A Study the menu on the lunch truck with your classmates and teacher.

B Write the information from the menu in the chart below.

Beverages	Sandwiches	Side orders

C Read the conversation. Then, practice the conversation changing the underlined words. Use the words from Exercise B.

Sebastien: Hi! I want a <u>ham sandwich</u>, please.
Server: Do you want a side order?
Sebastien: Yes, <u>a salad</u>.
Server: Great! Do you want a drink?
Sebastien: <u>Milk</u>, thanks.

GOAL ➤ **Place orders**

D Look at the menu. Talk to your classmates and teacher. What do you like to eat? What is cheap?

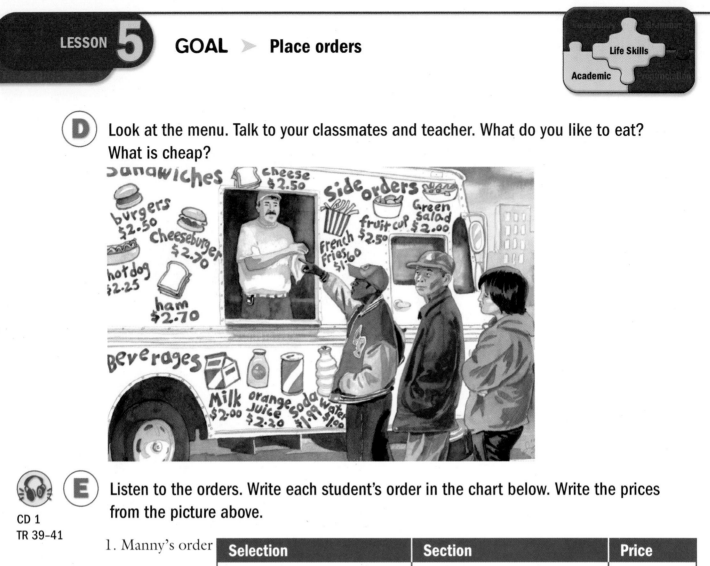

CD 1
TR 39–41

E Listen to the orders. Write each student's order in the chart below. Write the prices from the picture above.

1. Manny's order

Selection	Section	Price
soda	beverages	
cheeseburger	sandwiches	
green salad	side orders	
	Total	

2. Tran's order

Selection	Section	Price
	Total	

3. Miyuki's order

Selection	Section	Price
	Total	

F Study the chart with your classmates and teacher.

Questions and *Yes/No* Answers		
Question	**Yes**	**No**
Do you want a hamburger?	Yes, I do.	No, I don't. Thank you.
Do they want sandwiches?	Yes, they do.	No, they don't.
Does he want a sandwich?	Yes, he does.	No, he doesn't.
Does she want a hot dog?	Yes, she does.	No, she doesn't.

G Read the orders.

Sebastien

Sandwich: ham sandwich
Side order: salad
Beverage: milk

Tri

Sandwich: cheeseburger
Side order: french fries
Beverage: milk

Natalia

Sandwich: hot dog
Side order: french fries
Beverage: orange juice

H Answer the questions.

1. Does Sebastien want a salad? _____ Yes, he does. _____
2. Does Natalia want orange juice? _____
3. Do Sebastien and Tri want orange juice? _____
4. Do Sebastien and Tri want milk? _____
5. Do Tri and Natalia want ham sandwiches? _____
6. Does Natalia want a cheeseburger? _____

I Look at the menu on page 53. Write your order. Then, practice taking an order with a partner. Use the conversation in Exercise C on page 53 as a model.

Selection	Section	Price

J **Active Task.** Go to a lunch truck or cafeteria and order your lunch in English.

A Write the names of the foods and drinks above in the chart. Are they for breakfast, lunch, or dinner? Add more foods to each list. (Lessons 1–5)

Breakfast	Lunch	Dinner

B Talk to a partner about what he or she eats. Write the information. (Lessons 1–5)

1. What do you eat for breakfast? _____

2. What do you eat for lunch? _____

3. What do you eat for dinner? _____

C Write what you like to eat. (Lessons 1–5)

Breakfast	Lunch	Dinner

D Complete the sentences. (Lesson 1)

1. I _____ like toast _____ for breakfast.

2. My partner _____ for breakfast.

3. I _____ for lunch.

4. My partner _____ for lunch.

5. I _____ for dinner.

6. My partner _____ for dinner.

E Read the advertisement. (Lesson 2)

F Complete the chart. Use the information from Exercise E. (Lesson 2)

Product	Container or Quantity	Price
bread		
ground beef		
jelly		
cucumbers		
spaghetti		
cookies		
milk		
potato chips		

G Ask a partner questions about the advertisement in Exercise E. Ask: *How much is . . .?* or *How much are . . .?* (Lesson 2)

H Look at Sebastien's shopping list. What does he need? Write sentences. (Lesson 3)

SHOPPING LIST

6 bottles of water

1 jar of peanut butter

2 pounds of tomatoes

1 gallon of milk

1. Sebastien _____ six bottles of water.

2. _____

3. _____

4. _____

Rudolf's Café Lunch Menu

SANDWICHES
Ham...$2.75
Tuna..$2.75
Hamburger....................................$3.50

SIDE ORDERS
Salad...$1.98
Soup..$1.75
French fries..................................$1.50

BEVERAGES
Soda..$1.50
Milk...$1.00
Coffee...$1.50

ALLEN'S HOME COOKING
Lunch Menu

SANDWICHES
Turkey..$3.50
Cheese.......................................$2.25
Hamburger..................................$3.95

SIDE ORDERS
Salad..$2.75
French fries.................................$1.95

BEVERAGES
Soda...$2.00
Milk..$1.25
Coffee..$2.00

I Read the menu. Circle *R* for Rudolf's Café or *A* for Allen's Home Cooking. (Lessons 4 and 5)

1. Which is cheaper—a hamburger at Rudolf's Café or at Allen's Home Cooking?   R   A

2. Which is more expensive—a salad at Rudolf's or at Allen's?   R   A

3. Which is cheaper—coffee at Rudolf's or at Allen's?   R   A

4. Which is more expensive—soda at Rudolf's or at Allen's?   R   A

J Answer the questions about you and a partner. (Lesson 5)

1. Do you like pizza? _____ Yes, I do. _____

2. Do you eat hamburgers? _____

3. Do you eat egg rolls? _____

4. Do you make tuna fish sandwiches? _____

5. Does your partner like pizza? _____

6. Does your partner eat hamburgers? _____

7. Does your partner eat egg rolls? _____

8. Does your partner make tuna fish sandwiches? _____

My Dictionary

Make flash cards to improve your vocabulary.

1. Choose four new words from this unit.

2. Write each word on an index card or on a sheet of paper.

3. On the back of the index card or paper, draw a picture, find and write a sentence from the book with the word, and write the page number.

4. Study the words.

He needs four <u>bottles</u> of water.
page 48

Learner Log

Circle how well you learned each item and write the page number where you learned it.

1. I can name different foods for different meals.

   Yes   Maybe   No   Page _____

2. I can read advertisements.

   Yes   Maybe   No   Page _____

3. I can express needs and quantities.

   Yes   Maybe   No   Page _____

4. I can compare prices.

   Yes   Maybe   No   Page _____

5. I can read a menu.

   Yes   Maybe   No   Page _____

Rank what you like to do best from 1 to 6. 1 is your favorite activity. Your teacher will help you.

_____ Practice listening

_____ Practice speaking

_____ Practice reading

_____ Practice writing

_____ Learn new words

_____ Learn grammar

In the next unit, I want to practice more

_____ .

Team Project

Create a menu for a new restaurant.

In this project, you will create a menu for a new restaurant (including foods and prices) and an advertisement for your restaurant. You will also write a conversation between a server and customers in your restaurant as the server takes their orders.

1. Form a team with four or five students. In your team, you need:

POSITION	JOB	STUDENT NAME
Student 1: **Team Leader**	See that everyone speaks English. See that everyone participates.	
Student 2: **Advertising Agent**	With help from the team, make an advertisement for your restaurant with a few prices.	
Student 3: **Chef**	With help from the team, write a list of foods for the menu. Design the menu.	
Students 4/5: **Trainers**	With help from the team, write a conversation between a server and customers in a restaurant.	

2. Choose a name for your restaurant.

3. Make a list of foods your restaurant serves.

4. Design a menu.

5. Create an advertisement for your restaurant, giving some prices.

6. Create a conversation.

7. Present your conversation and menu to the class.

8. Compare prices on your menu with prices from other teams' menus.

UNIT 4 Housing

GOALS

➤ Identify types of housing

➤ Describe parts of a home

➤ Interpret classified ads

➤ Use the telephone and make appointments

➤ Identify furniture in a house

LESSON 1

A house or an apartment?

GOAL ➤ Identify types of housing

Vocabulary · Grammar · Life Skills · Academic · Pronunciation

A Study the pie chart about housing in Corbin. Listen and write the numbers.

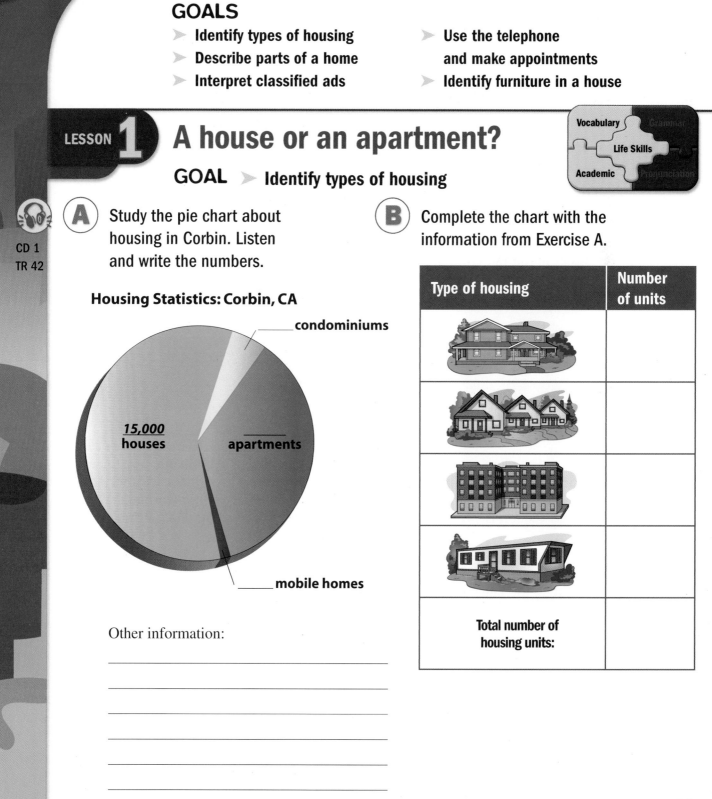

Housing Statistics: Corbin, CA

condominiums

_15,000_ houses

_____ apartments

_____ mobile homes

Other information:

_____

_____

_____

_____

_____

_____

B Complete the chart with the information from Exercise A.

Type of housing	Number of units
Total number of housing units:	

GOAL ➤ **Identify types of housing**

Grammar
Life Skills
Pronunciation

 Study the chart with your classmates and teacher.

Simple Present: *Live*		
Subject	**Verb**	**Example sentence**
I, you, we, they	live	I **live** in a house. You **live** in an apartment. We **live** in a condominium. They **live** in a mobile home.
he, she, it	lives	He **lives** in a house. She **lives** in an apartment.

Pronunciation

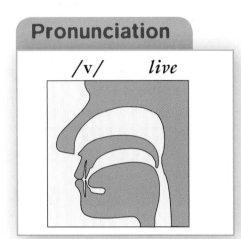

/v/   *live*

 Read about the students and their homes.

Saud

Silvia

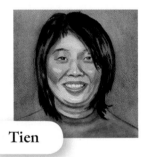

Tien

Housing: house
Address: 2323 Hartford Rd.
City: Corbin
State: California

Housing: mobile home
Address: 13 Palm Ave.
City: Corbin
State: California

Housing: apartment
Address: 15092 Arbor Lane #22
City: Corbin
State: California

E Practice the conversation with a partner. Then, make new conversations.

Saud: Do you live in a house, an apartment, or a condominium?
Tien: I live in <u>an apartment</u>.
Saud: Where do you live?
Tien: My address is <u>15092 Arbor Lane #22</u>.
Saud: Where does Silvia live?
Tien: She lives at <u>13 Palm Ave.</u>
Saud: That's close by.

a /an

a house
an apartment

F Read the paragraph.

Felipe is from Argentina. He lives in a condominium in Corbin, California. His brothers live in Los Angeles, California. They live in a small house.

G Copy the paragraph above onto a sheet of paper. Then, talk with a partner. Write a new paragraph about your partner.

H Ask four classmates what type of housing they live in. Complete the chart.

Name	Type of housing
Saud	Saud lives in a house.

I Complete the pie chart with the information from Exercise H.

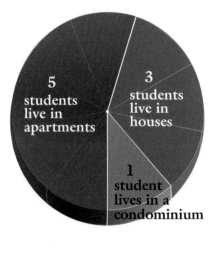

Does it have a yard?

GOAL ➤ Describe parts of a home

Where is Saud?
Why is he there?

A Look at the floor plan. Answer the questions.

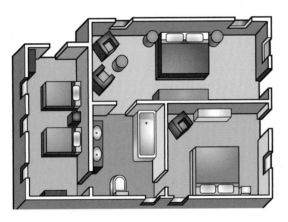

1. How many bedrooms are in the floor plan?

_____

2. How many bathrooms are there?

_____

B Listen to Saud and the real estate agent. How many bedrooms and bathrooms does Saud need? Then, listen to the other conversations and fill in the information.

CD 1
TR 43–46

Name	Number of bedrooms	Number of bathrooms
1. Saud		
2. Silvia		
3. Tien		
4. Felipe		

C Study the words with your classmates and teacher.

| bedroom | bathroom | kitchen | dining room | living room |

D Where in a home do people do these things? With a group, write the names of the rooms. Use the words from the box above.

Activity		Room
People sleep in this room.		bedroom
People take showers in this room.		
People watch TV in this room.		
People eat dinner in this room.		
People make dinner in this room.		

E Talk with a partner about rooms in a home.

EXAMPLE: *Student A:* Where do people make breakfast?
　　　　　Student B: People make breakfast in the kitchen.

1. Where do people sleep?

2. Where do people take showers?

3. Where do people watch TV?

4. Where do people eat dinner?

5. Where do people make dinner?

GOAL ➤ **Describe parts of a home**

F Study the picture. Write the correct letter next to each word.

_____ stairs   _____ swimming pool   _____ bathroom   _____ family room

_____ kitchen   _____ garage   _____ hall   _____ balcony

_____ bedroom   _____ deck   _____ front porch   _____ front yard

_____ backyard   _____ driveway

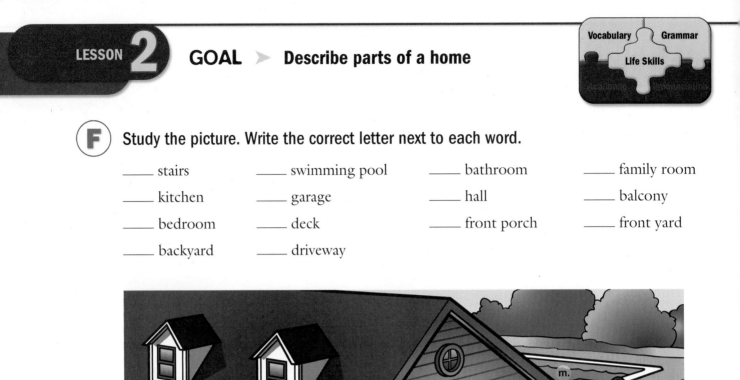

G Ask your partner about his or her home.

1. What kind of home do you have?
2. How many bedrooms do you have?
3. How many bathrooms do you have?
4. Do you have a front yard or backyard?
5. Do you have a garage or carport?
6. Do you have a balcony?

Verb: *Have*

I **have** . . .
He/She **has** . . .

carport

Look in the newspaper.

GOAL ➤ Interpret classified ads

Life Skills

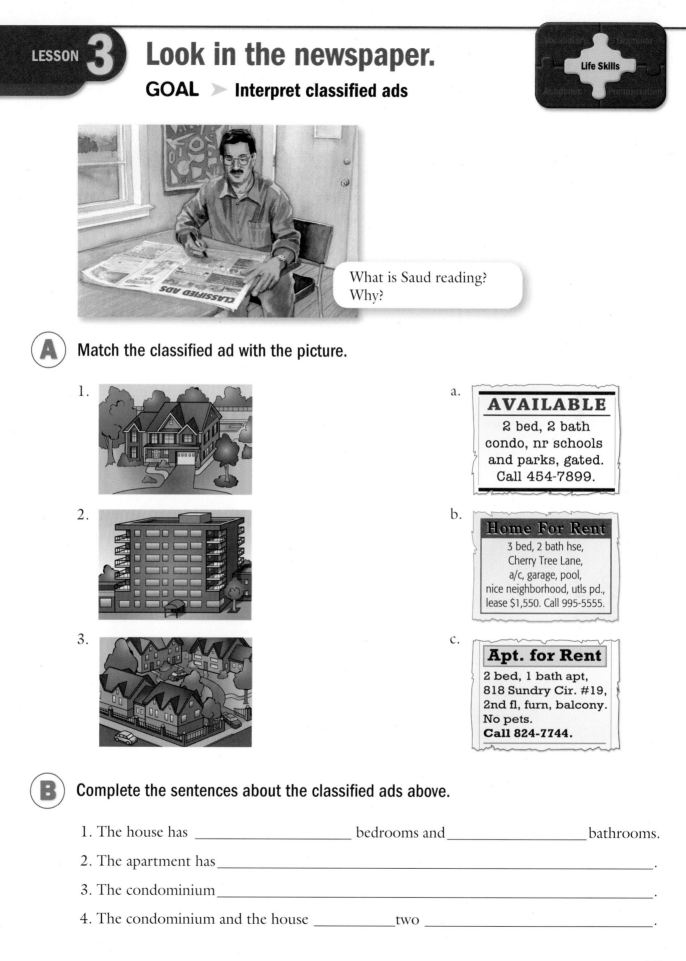

What is Saud reading?
Why?

A Match the classified ad with the picture.

1.

a.
AVAILABLE
2 bed, 2 bath
condo, nr schools
and parks, gated.
Call 454-7899.

2.

b.
Home For Rent
3 bed, 2 bath hse,
Cherry Tree Lane,
a/c, garage, pool,
nice neighborhood, utls pd.,
lease $1,550. Call 995-5555.

3.

c.
Apt. for Rent
2 bed, 1 bath apt,
818 Sundry Cir. #19,
2nd fl, furn, balcony.
No pets.
Call 824-7744.

B Complete the sentences about the classified ads above.

1. The house has _____ bedrooms and_____ bathrooms.

2. The apartment has_____.

3. The condominium_____.

4. The condominium and the house _____two _____.

Vocabulary   Grammar
Life Skills
Academic   Pronunciation

C Read the classified ad.

APT. FOR RENT
2 bed, 1 bath apt,
818 Sundry Ave., #13
$900, furn, a/c,
all utls pd, 1 mo dep.
Call 555-6294.

D Draw a line from the word to its abbreviation.

1. apartment   a. utls
2. furnished   b. dep
3. utilities   c. apt
4. air-conditioning   d. furn
5. paid   e. a/c
6. deposit   f. pd

Utilities:

gas

water

electricity

E Read the classified ads.

a. **FOR RENT**
3 bed, 2 bath apt.
a/c, balcony,
$800. Call Lien
at 555-1734.

b. **Apt. for Rent**
$700/MONTH
1 bed, 1 bath apt.
No pets.
Call Fred at
555-7164.

c. **FOR RENT**
2 bed, 3 bath apt.
a/c, elect. pd.
Call Margaret for
more information-
555-2672.

d. **AVAILABLE**
✪ 3 bed, ✪
3 bath apt.
w/pool, utls pd.,
nr school.
Call 555-5987.

F Listen and write the letter of the classified ad above.

CD 1
TR 47

1. _____

2. _____

3. _____

4. _____

LESSON 3 **GOAL** ➤ **Interpret classified ads**

 G Study the chart with your classmates and teacher.

Yes/No Questions	
Question	**Answer**
Does it have three bedrooms?	Yes, it does. No, it doesn't.
Does it have air-conditioning?	Yes, it does. No, it doesn't.

Pronunciation

Intonation: *Yes/No* Questions

➤ Does it have three bedrooms?

➤ Does it have air-conditioning?

H Read the classified ad and answer the questions.

FOR RENT-CONDO
3 bed, 2 bath condo,
22954 Kensington Place,
a/c, utls pd., lrg yard,
$1,500 a month.
Call Margaret: 555-3452

1. Does the home have four bedrooms? _____

2. Does it have a yard? _____

3. Does it have two bathrooms? _____

4. Does it have furniture? _____

5. Does it have a balcony? _____

I Put a check (✓) by things in your home.

_____ pets allowed _____ utilities paid _____ balcony _____ garage
_____ air-conditioning _____ near a school _____ near a park

J Write a classified ad about your home.

 K **Active Task.** Look in a newspaper or on the Internet to find a home that is good for your family.

When can I see it?

GOAL ➤ Use the telephone and make appointments

What is Saud doing?
Who is he talking to?

 A Read about Saud.

Saud needs a new apartment. He follows four steps:
1. He talks to a rental agent.
2. He reads classified ads.
3. He calls for appointments.
4. He looks at homes.

 B Match the questions with the answers. Then, listen and check your answers.

CD 1
TR 48

1. How much is the rent?   a. It is quiet and there is a school nearby.

2. How is the neighborhood?   b. Today at 3:00.

3. When can I see the apartment?   c. It's $1,200 a month.

4. Does it have air-conditioning? d. Yes, they are.

5. Are pets OK?   e. Yes, it does.

LESSON 4 **GOAL** ➤ **Use the telephone and make appointments**

 C Practice the conversation.

Owner: Hello, can I help you?
Saud: Yes, I am calling about the condominium for rent.
Owner: How can I help you?
Saud: How much is the rent?
Owner: It's $1,200 a month.
Saud: When can I see it?
Owner: How about today at 3:00?
Saud: Great! Thank you.

 D Listen to the conversations. Complete the chart.

CD 1
TR 49–52

	How much is the rent?	What time is the appointment?
1.	$1,200	3:00
2.		
3.		
4.		

E Complete Conversation 2 with the information from Exercise D.

Owner: Hello. Can I help you?
Saud: Yes, I am calling about the apartment for rent that I saw in the paper. Is it still available?
Owner: Yes, we are renting it for _____.
Saud: Wow! That sounds expensive.
Owner: Maybe, but it is a beautiful and new apartment.
Saud: OK, when can I see it?
Owner: You can stop by at _____.

 F Practice Conversations 3 and 4 with the information from Exercise D.

GOAL ➤ Use the telephone
and make appointments

G Study the chart with your classmates and teacher.

Present Continuous			
Subject	***Be* Verb**	**Base + *ing***	**Example sentence**
I	am	talk + *ing*	I **am talking** on the phone.
you, we, they	are	read+ *ing* call + *ing*	We **are calling** for an appointment.
he, she, it	is	move + *ing*	She **is moving** into a new apartment.

H Write sentences in the present continuous. What is Saud doing?

1. Saud _____ to a rental agent.

2. He _____.

3. He _____.

I Complete the sentences with the present continuous.

1. I _____ am reading _____ the classified ads.

2. They _____ into a new home.

3. We _____ at a condominium.

4. Silvia _____ for an appointment.

5. You _____ on the phone.

J In a group, rank the steps 1–4. The step that is most important is 1.

_____ He talks to a rental agent.   _____ He calls for appointments.

_____ He reads classified ads.   _____ He looks at homes.

Where do you want the sofa?

GOAL ➤ Identify furniture in a house

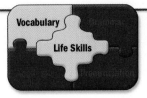

Vocabulary
Life Skills

A Write the words under the correct room. Share your ideas with a partner.

1. bed   2. car   3. chair   4. refrigerator   5. bathtub   6. sofa

1. bedroom _____   3. dining room _____   5. garage _____

2. kitchen _____   4. bathroom _____   6. living room _____

B In a group, list the other things you see in the rooms above. Use a dictionary or ask your teacher for help.

Bedroom	Kitchen	Dining room	Bathroom	Garage	Living room

GOAL ➤ **Identify furniture in a house**

Vocabulary Grammar
Life Skills
Academics Pronunciation

C Study the prepositions with your classmates and teacher.

in   on   under

over   next to   between

D Ask a partner where things are in the pictures above. Ask about *the lamp*, *the cat*, *the nightstand*, *the sofa*, and *the clock*.

EXAMPLE: *Student A:* Where's the trash?
          Student B: It's in the trash can.

E Use prepositions to say the location of things in your classroom. Your partner will guess which thing you are talking about.

EXAMPLE: *Student A:* It's next to the window.
          Student B: The TV?

GOAL ➤ **Identify furniture in a house**

F Study the words with your classmates and teacher.

a window

a door

an end table

a coffee table

a dining room chair

a painting

a lamp

 G Look at the living room. Follow the instructions.

CD 1
TR 53

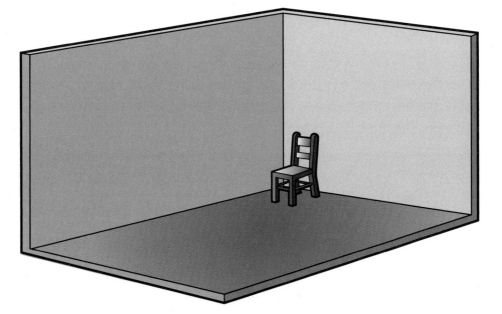

H Show your partner where the furniture is in your classroom. Walk around the room and talk about it.

 I **Active Task.** Find a picture of a room with furniture from a magazine or on the Internet. Show the picture to the class and describe it.

Review

A Read the classified ads. (Lesson 3)

NewsObserver Sunday, October

❶ HOUSE FOR RENT

2 bed, 2 bath hse.
all utls pd, large 2-car
garage, lge backyard.
$1,450 a month.
Call Pat to see:
555-3444

❹ FOR RENT

Mobile home nr schools,
1st month rent paid,
all utls pd, 2 bed, 1 bath,
no pets, pool.
Good management,
$650.
Call Jackie
555-1301

APT. FOR

❷ APT. FOR RENT

3 bed, 1 bath apt.
2nd floor, balcony,
furn., no pets, nr park
and recreation.
$800 lease.
Call Pedro 555-3467.

➡ **NEW LISTING** ⬅

❺ FOR RENT

1 bed, 1 bath apt.
nr college, carport,
$600. Call 555-4454.

➡ **NEW LISTING** ⬅

HOUSE FOR RENT

New construction on
nr park

❸ CONDO FOR RENT

CONDO,
2 bed, 1 bath, utls pd,
pool and spa, a/c.
$950.
555-5877

❻ HOUSE FOR RENT

5395 Raymond Circle.
Beautiful house.
2 bed, 1 bath,
garage.
$1,500.
Call Eva 555-5600.

APT. FOR RENT

Spacious 5 b 4 bath
a   t w

B Cover the classified ads above so you can't see them. Ask your partner questions about the ads and write the information below. Then, your partner covers the ads and asks questions. (Lessons 1–3)

What kind of housing is it?	How many bedrooms are there?	How many bathrooms are there?	Is it near anything?	How much is the rent?
1. house				
2.			park	
3.	2			
4.				
5.		1		
6.				$1,500

C Study the words. Complete the chart with the words. (Lessons 2 and 5)

| kitchen | pool | hall | sofa | bathtub |
| balcony | porch | driveway | deck | refrigerator |

Inside	Outside

D Look at the picture and complete the sentences. (Lesson 5)

1. The cat is _____ the sofa.

2. The lamp is _____ the sofa.

3. The sofa is _____ the end table and the lamp.

4. The book is _____ the _____.

5. The painting is _____ the sofa.

Review

E Describe the pictures with sentences in the present continuous. (Lesson 4)

Carmen

Saud

Saud

1. Carmen _____.

2. Saud _____.

3. Saud _____.

F Write a conversation about finding a home. Make an appointment to see the home. (Lesson 4)

Owner: _____

You: _____

Owner: _____

You: _____

Owner: _____

You: _____

Owner: _____

You: _____

G List furniture for each room. (Lesson 5)

Bedroom	Kitchen	Dining room	Bathroom	Garage	Living room

My Dictionary

Make flash cards to improve your vocabulary.

1. Choose four new words from this unit.

2. Write each word on an index card or on a sheet of paper.

3. On the back of the index card or paper, draw a picture, find and write a sentence from the book with the word, and write the page number.

4. Study the words.

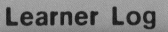

Do you have a garage or a carport?

page 66

Learner Log

Circle how well you learned each item and write the page number where you learned it.

1. I can name different types of housing.

   Yes   Maybe   No   Page _____

2. I can name parts of a home.

   Yes   Maybe   No   Page _____

3. I can read classified ads.

   Yes   Maybe   No   Page _____

4. I can find a home to rent.

   Yes   Maybe   No   Page _____

5. I can name types of furniture.

   Yes   Maybe   No   Page _____

Rank what you like to do best from 1 to 6. 1 is your favorite activity. Your teacher will help you.

_____ Practice listening

_____ Practice speaking

_____ Practice reading

_____ Practice writing

_____ Learn new words

_____ Learn grammar

In the next unit, I want to practice more

_____ .

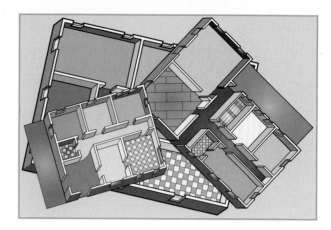

Plan a dream home.

In this project, you will make a floor plan of a dream home, write a classified ad for the home, and present both to the class.

1. Form a team with four or five students. In your team, you need:

POSITION	JOB	STUDENT NAME
Student 1: **Team Leader**	See that everyone speaks English. See that everyone participates.	
Student 2: **Architect**	With help from the team, draw the floor plan.	
Student 3: **Decorator**	With help from the team, place furniture in your plan.	
Students 4/5: **Spokespeople**	With help from the team, organize a presentation.	

2. Choose a kind of home. Is it an apartment, house, condominium, or mobile home?

3. Make a floor plan of the home.

4. Make a list of furniture for your home.

5. Decide where to put the furniture.

6. Write a classified ad for your home.

7. Plan a presentation for the class and present your dream home.

UNIT 5

Our Community

GOALS

➤ Identify locations and services

➤ Give and follow street directions

➤ Give and follow directions in a mall

➤ Leave phone messages

➤ Write a message on a postcard

LESSON 1 **Places and services**

GOAL ➤ Identify locations and services

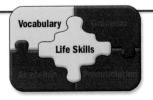

A Look at the Web page with your classmates and teacher. Talk about the different sections.

B List the government agencies and services.

1. _____public libraries_____   4. _____

2. _____   5. _____

3. _____   6. _____

C Work in a group. Write the words from the box under the correct pictures below.

apartment	hostel	hotel	dentist's office
tennis court	hospital	motel	doctor's office
mobile home	playground	house	park

Imperatives

Put hotel under *Lodging*.

Add hotel to *Lodging*.

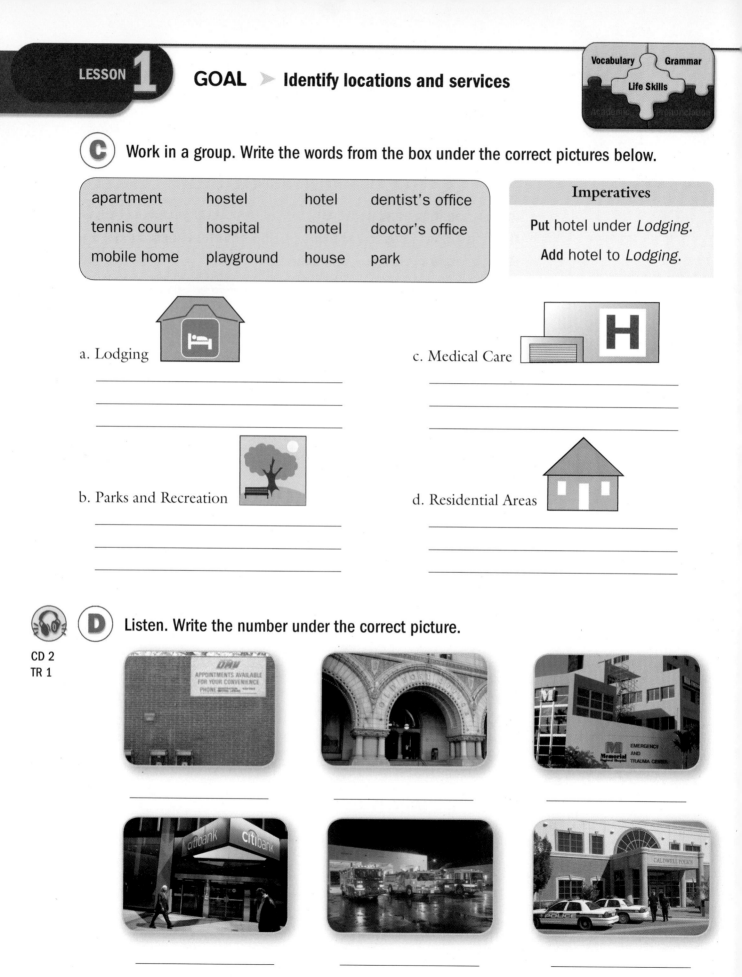

a. Lodging

_____

_____

_____

b. Parks and Recreation

_____

_____

_____

c. Medical Care

_____

_____

_____

d. Residential Areas

_____

_____

_____

D Listen. Write the number under the correct picture.

CD 2
TR 1

_____   _____   _____

_____   _____   _____

What are they doing?
Who are they calling?

 E   **Listen to the conversation. Practice the conversation with new information.**

CD 2
TR 2

Emanuela: I need to call the <u>hospital</u>.
Lisa: Why?
Emanuela: <u>My sister is very sick</u>.
Lisa: The number is <u>555-7665</u>.

Place	Problem	Phone number
hospital	My sister is very sick.	555-7665
bank	I need to get some money from my account.	555-4856
DMV	I need a driver's license.	555-7698
post office	I need to send a letter.	555-2047

F   **Make a bar graph for your class. How many students go to these places?**

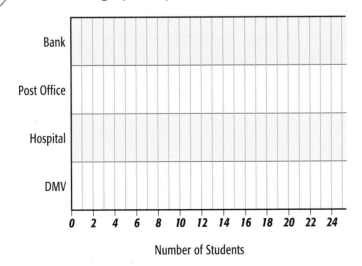

Number of Students

 G   **Active Task.** Find a telephone directory or look on the Internet. Make a list of important numbers to put by your phone at home.

Where is City Hall?

GOAL ➤ Give and follow street directions

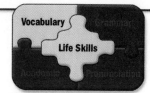

 A Practice the conversation.

Alma: I need to find City Hall.
Gabriela: Of course. Go straight ahead one block and turn right.
Alma: That's straight ahead one block and turn right?
Gabriela: Yes. It's on the left.
Alma: Thanks.
Gabriela: No problem.

Where is Gabriela? What is she doing?

B Practice these phrases with your classmates and teacher.

turn left	turn right
go straight ahead	turn around

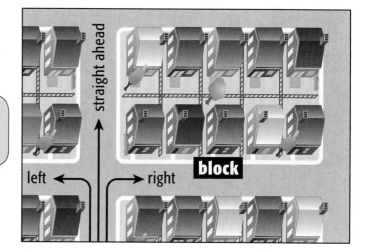

C With a partner, make new conversations. Use Exercise A as a model.

Place	Directions
1. bus station	Go straight ahead one block and turn right. Go one block and turn right. Go one block. It's on the left.
2. City Hall	Go straight ahead one block and turn right. It's on the left.
3. Rosco's Buffet Restaurant	Go straight ahead two blocks and turn left. It's on the right.
4. the post office	Go straight ahead one block and turn right. Go one more block and turn left. It's on the right.
5. the zoo	Go straight ahead two blocks and turn right. It's on the right.
6. the high school	Go straight ahead two blocks and turn right. Go one more block and turn right. It's on the left.

GOAL ➤ **Give and follow street directions**

D Look at the map. Read the directions from Exercise C on page 84. Number the places 1–6 in the squares on the map.

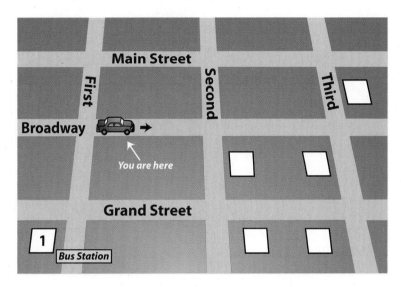

E Where are the places? Look at the map and complete the table.

Place	Location
1. the bus station	The bus station is on Grand Street.
2. City Hall	
3. Rosco's Buffet Restaurant	
4. the post office	
5. the zoo	
6. the high school	

F Practice the conversation with a partner.

Student A: Where is the bus station?
Student B: It's on Grand Street in Landsbury.

in / on

in the city

on the street

It's *on* Main Street *in* Landsbury.

GOAL ⟩ Give and follow street directions

G Write the phrases under the signs.

| Turn right | Turn left | Turn around | Go straight |

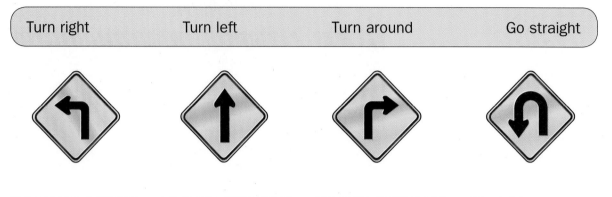

_____   _____   _____   _____

 H Listen and check (✓) the boxes for the phrases you hear.

CD 2
TR 3-7

	Turn right	Turn left	Turn around	Go straight
1. Directions to the mall	✓		✓	✓
2. Directions to the post office				
3. Directions to the movie theater				
4. Directions to the museum				
5. Directions to the park				

I Ask four classmates and complete the chart.

EXAMPLE: *Student A:* Where do you live, Herman?
　　　　　Student B: I live <u>in</u> Landsbury <u>on</u> Maple Avenue.

Student name	City	Street
Herman	Landsbury	Maple Avenue
1.		
2.		
3.		
4.		

Let's go to the mall!

GOAL ➤ Give and follow directions in a mall

Life Skills
Academic

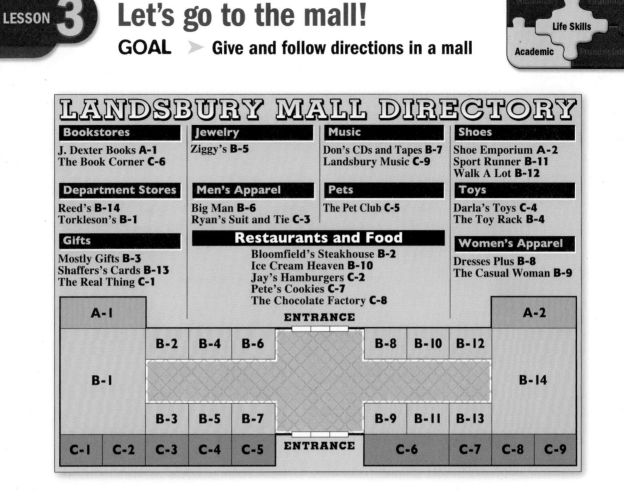

LANDSBURY MALL DIRECTORY

Bookstores	**Jewelry**	**Music**	**Shoes**
J. Dexter Books **A-1** The Book Corner **C-6**	Ziggy's **B-5**	Don's CDs and Tapes **B-7** Landsbury Music **C-9**	Shoe Emporium **A-2** Sport Runner **B-11** Walk A Lot **B-12**

Department Stores	**Men's Apparel**	**Pets**	**Toys**
Reed's **B-14** Torkleson's **B-1**	Big Man **B-6** Ryan's Suit and Tie **C-3**	The Pet Club **C-5**	Darla's Toys **C-4** The Toy Rack **B-4**

Gifts	**Restaurants and Food**	**Women's Apparel**
Mostly Gifts **B-3** Shaffers's Cards **B-13** The Real Thing **C-1**	Bloomfield's Steakhouse **B-2** Ice Cream Heaven **B-10** Jay's Hamburgers **C-2** Pete's Cookies **C-7** The Chocolate Factory **C-8**	Dresses Plus **B-8** The Casual Woman **B-9**

A-1   ENTRANCE   A-2

B-2 B-4 B-6   B-8 B-10 B-12

B-1   B-14

B-3 B-5 B-7   B-9 B-11 B-13

C-1 C-2 C-3 C-4 C-5 ENTRANCE C-6   C-7 C-8 C-9

 A Answer the questions about the directory.

1. What store is next to Big Man? _____

2. What store is next to Dresses Plus? _____

3. What store is between The Pet Club and Ryan's Suit and Tie? _____

4. What store is between Landsbury Music and Pete's Cookies? _____

B Scan the directory. Take turns asking and answering the following questions with a partner.

1. Where can you buy a dog?

2. Where can you buy a suit for a man?

3. Where can you buy ice cream?

4. Where can you buy sneakers?

5. Where can you eat a steak?

LESSON **3**

GOAL ➤ **Give and follow directions in a mall**

C Study the directory with your classmates and teacher. Listen for prepositions.

CD 2
TR 8

| J. Dexter Books | | | | | | Shoe Emporium |

```
ENTRANCE

Bloom-field's Steak-house | The Toy Rack | Big Man        Dresses Plus | Ice Cream Heaven | Walk A Lot

Torkleson's                                                Reed's

            Mostly Gifts | Ziggy's | Don's CDs and Tapes    The Casual Woman | Sport Runner | Shaffer's Cards

                                         ENTRANCE

The Real Thing | Jay's Ham-burgers | Ryan's Suit and Tie | Darla's Toys | The Pet Club      The Book Corner | Pete's Cookies | The Chocolate Factory | Lands-bury Music
```

around the corner   next to   on the corner   between   across from

D Write sentences about the mall. Follow the examples.

1. Ziggy's is around the corner from Pet Club. _____

2. _____

3. The Casual Woman is across from Dresses Plus. _____

4. _____

5. Landsbury Music is on the corner. _____

6. _____

7. Sport Runner is between Shaffer's Cards and The Casual Woman. ____

8. _____

9. The Book Corner is next to Pete's Cookies. _____

10. _____

88   Unit 5   Lesson 3

J. Dexter Books							

ENTRANCE

| Torkleson's | The Toy Rack | Big Man | | Dresses Plus | Walk A Lot | | Reed's |

| Mostly Gifts | Ziggy's | Don's CDs and Tapes | | The Casual Woman | Shaffer's Cards |

ENTRANCE

| Jay's Ham-burgers | Ryan's Suit and Tie | Darla's Toys | | The Book Corner | Pete's Cookies | The Chocolate Factory | Lands-bury Music |

E   Student A: Cover page 88 and ask Student B where Ice Cream Heaven, Shoe Emporium, and The Pet Club are. Write the information in the floor plan.

EXAMPLE: Where's Ice Cream Heaven?

F   Student B: Cover page 88 and ask Student A where Sport Runner, Real Thing, and Bloomfield's Steakhouse are. Write the information in the floor plan.

G   In groups create a mall directory and floor plan.

Please call.

GOAL ➤ Leave phone messages

Who is the package from?
Who is the package to?

A Read about Gabriela's problem.

Gabriela has a problem. She needs to go to the post office. She wants to send a package to her family in Buenos Aires, Argentina. She doesn't know what to say at the post office.

B What can Gabriela do? Who can help her? Talk in a group and complete the sentences below.

1. She can ask _____.

2. She can call _____.

3. She can go _____.

CD 2
TR 9

C Listen to Gabriela leave a message. Circle the answers.

1. Who does she talk to?

    a. her friend David

    b. a machine

    c. David, her brother

2. When does she want to go to the post office?

    a. today

    b. tomorrow

    c. Saturday

GOAL ➤ **Leave phone messages**

D There are three important parts of a message. Read the chart with your classmates and teacher.

Your name	Reason for calling	Your phone number
Gabriela	I have a question.	My number is 555-2344.
	I want to talk.	Call me at 555-2344.
	I need some information.	Can you call me back at 555-2344?

E Look at the messages. Talk in a group. Circle the good messages.

1. This is Gabriela. I need help. I want to send a package. Please call me at 555-2344. Thanks.

2. Call me. OK?

3. I am Gabriela. My phone number is 555-2344.

4. This is your friend Gabriela from school. My number is 555-2344. Please call me. I have a question for you. Thanks.

5. This is Gabriela. My number is 555-2344. I have a small problem. Can you call me back? Thanks.

F Practice leaving a message with two classmates. Student A writes the information.

EXAMPLE: *Student A:* Hello, this is Gabriela. I can't come to the phone right now. Please leave a message.

  Student B: This is Ramon. I have a question. My number is 555-2125.

Name: _____	**Name:** _____
Phone number: _____	**Phone number:** _____
Reason for calling: _____	**Reason for calling:** _____
_____	_____

LESSON 4 **GOAL** ➤ **Leave phone messages**

G Study the chart with your classmates and teacher.

Questions with *Can*			
Can	**Subject**	**Base verb**	**Example question**
can	I you	help ask talk answer call	**Can** I help you? **Can** I ask you a question? **Can** I talk to you? **Can** you answer a question? **Can** you call me?

H Match the questions with the responses. There may be more than one correct response.

1. Can you help me?

2. Can I ask you a question?

3. Can I talk to you?

4. Can you answer a question?

5. Can you call me?

a. Yes. What's the question?

b. I can call you tomorrow.

c. Sure. What can I do for you?

d. OK. What can we talk about?

e. Yes. What's the question?

 I Write questions. Put the words in the correct order.

1. help / can / I / you   _____Can I help you?_____

2. answer / the question / I / can   _____

3. I / talk / to you / can / tomorrow   _____

4. I / can / you / see / tomorrow   _____

J Write a message you can leave for a friend on an answering machine for each situation.

I am very sick. _____

I have a problem. _____

I don't understand. _____

Dear Mom

GOAL ➤ Write a message on a postcard

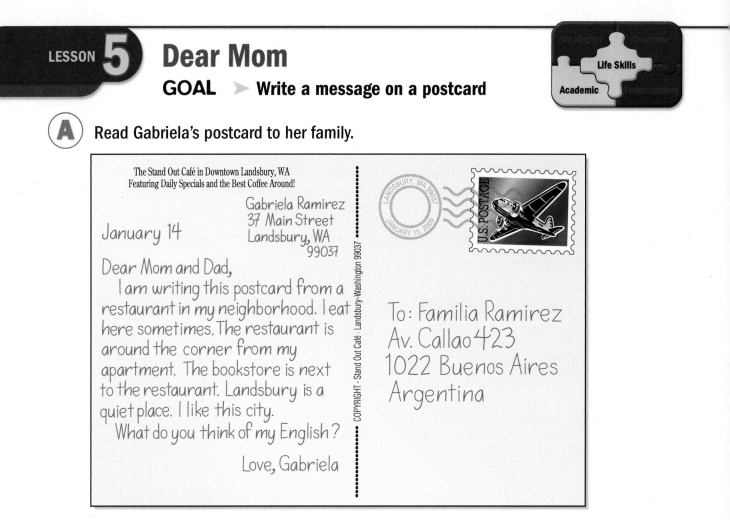

A Read Gabriela's postcard to her family.

*The Stand Out Café in Downtown Landsbury, WA
Featuring Daily Specials and the Best Coffee Around!*

January 14

Gabriela Ramirez
37 Main Street
Landsbury, WA
99037

Dear Mom and Dad,
  I am writing this postcard from a restaurant in my neighborhood. I eat here sometimes. The restaurant is around the corner from my apartment. The bookstore is next to the restaurant. Landsbury is a quiet place. I like this city.
  What do you think of my English?

          Love, Gabriela

COPYRIGHT - Stand Out Café - Landsbury-Washington 99037

To: Familia Ramirez
Av. Callao 423
1022 Buenos Aires
Argentina

B Answer the questions about the postcard.

1. What is Gabriela's address?

   _____

2. What is her family's address?

   _____

3. Where is the bookstore?

   _____

4. When did she write the postcard?

   _____

5. Who is the postcard to?

   _____

6. Where is Gabriela writing the letter from?

   _____

C Study the charts with your classmates and teacher.

Present Continuous				
Subject	**Be**	**Base + ing**	**Time**	**Example sentence**
I	am (I'm)	writing	right now today	I'm **writing** a letter right now.
he, she, it	is (she's)	eating		She's **eating** a sandwich.
you, we, they	are (they're)	reading		They're **reading** a book today.

Simple Present			
Subject	**Adverb**	**Verb**	**Example sentence**
I	always often	write	I always **write** postcards.
he, she, it	sometimes	eats	He rarely **eats** here.
you, we, they	rarely never	read	They never **read** the newspaper.

Adverbs of Frequency

0%	50%	100%

never	rarely	sometimes	usually	always

D Complete the sentences with the present continuous form of the verb in parentheses.

1. She _____is eating_____ (eat) at a restaurant.

2. They _____ (write) postcards.

3. We _____ (read) postcards.

4. I _____ (go) to the hospital. I am very sick.

5. Gabriela _____ (buy) a book at the bookstore right now.

write ➙ writing

E Complete the sentences with the simple present form of the verb in parentheses.

1. She _____lives_____ (live) in Landsbury.

2. I never _____ (read) classified ads.

3. We rarely _____ (study) on Saturday.

4. They often _____ (write) postcards at lunchtime.

5. You _____ (go) to school at Orangewood School for Adults.

study ➙ studies

F   **Listen and answer the questions.**

1. Where do you go to school? <u>I go to</u> _____ .

2. Where do you live? <u>I live</u> _____ .

3. Where is a restaurant nearby? <u>A restaurant is</u> _____ .

4. What do you sometimes do? <u>I sometimes</u> _____ .

G   **Ask a partner questions and write his or her answers.**

1. Where do you go to school?

<u>He (She) goes to</u> _____ .

2. Where do you live?

_____ .

3. Where is a restaurant nearby?

_____ .

4. What do you sometimes do?

_____ .

H   **Write a postcard to a family member about your city. Use the ideas from this page.**

The Stand Out Café in Downtown Landsbury, WA
Featuring Daily Specials and the Best Coffee Around!

COPYRIGHT · Stand Out Café · Landsbury-Washington 99037

PLACE STAMP
HERE

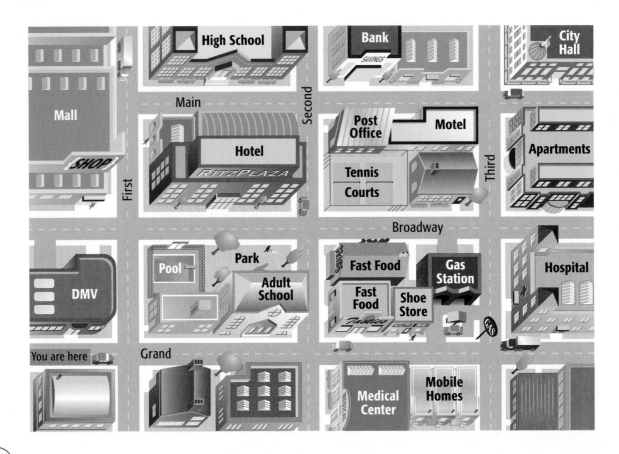

Review

A Look at the map. Ask a partner for directions to these places. (Lessons 1 and 2)

the motel	the mobile homes	the hospital
the park	the apartments	the hotel
the public pool	the dentist	the post office

EXAMPLE: *Student A:* Where are the tennis courts?
Student B: They are on Second Street, next to the post office.

B Give directions to a partner to each location. (Lesson 2)

the hotel	the apartments	City Hall
the dentist	the hospital	the high school
the bank	the motel	the DMV

EXAMPLE: *Student A:* Can you give me directions to the medical center?
Student B: Yes, go straight ahead on Grand. Go one block. It's on the right.

CD 2
TR 11

C Listen to the messages. Complete the chart. (Lesson 4)

Name	Reason for calling	Phone number
1. Nadia	I have a question.	555-2134
2. Vien		
3. David		
4. Ricardo		

D Write sentences about yourself. (Lesson 5)

I always _____.

I often _____.

Sometimes I _____.

I rarely _____.

I never _____.

E With a group, list the types of stores you can find at a mall. (Lesson 3)

_____   _____

_____   _____

_____   _____

_____   _____

_____   _____

Review

F   Read the services in the box. Then, write them under the correct places below. (Lesson 1)

a. Delivers mail   b. Helps sick people   c. Keeps your money safe   d. Gives licenses

1.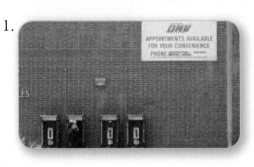

_____

3.

_____

2.

_____

4.

_____

G   Write a new postcard. Use the model on page 93. (Lesson 5)

The Stand Out Café in Downtown Landsbury, WA
Featuring Daily Specials and the Best Coffee Around!

COPYRIGHT - Stand Out Café · Landsbury-Washington 99037

PLACE STAMP
HERE

My Dictionary

Make flash cards to improve your vocabulary.

1. Choose four new words from this unit.

2. Write each word on an index card or on a sheet of paper.

3. On the back of the index card or paper, draw a picture, find and write a sentence from the book with the word, and write the page number.

4. Study the words.

Go straight ahead one block and turn right.

page 84

Learner Log

Circle how well you learned each item and write the page number where you learned it.

1. I can list places and services.

   Yes   Maybe   No   Page _____

2. I can give and follow street directions.

   Yes   Maybe   No   Page _____

3. I can follow directions in a mall.

   Yes   Maybe   No   Page _____

4. I can leave a phone message.

   Yes   Maybe   No   Page _____

5. I can write a postcard in English.

   Yes   Maybe   No   Page _____

Rank what you like to do best from 1 to 6. 1 is your favorite activity. Your teacher will help you.

_____ Practice listening

_____ Practice speaking

_____ Practice reading

_____ Practice writing

_____ Learn new words

_____ Learn grammar

In the next unit, I want to practice more

_____.

Team Project

Make a brochure of a new city.

In this project, you will make a brochure of a new city and present it to the class.

1. Form a team with four or five students. In your team, you need:

POSITION	JOB	STUDENT NAME
Student 1: **Team Leader**	See that everyone speaks English. See that everyone participates.	
Student 2: **City Planner**	With help from the team, draw a map of your city.	
Student 3: **Artist**	With help from the team, make a brochure of your city.	
Students 4/5: **Spokespeople**	With help from the team, organize a presentation to give to the class.	

2. Choose a name for your city.

3. Make a list of important places in your city and put them in alphabetical order.

4. Make a map of your city and mark where the important places are.

5. Make a brochure. On the brochure, write one paragraph about the city, write the names of your team's members, and draw a picture that represents the city.

6. Prepare a presentation for the class.

Health and Fitness

GOALS

➤ **Identify parts of the body**
➤ **Identify illnesses**
   and health problems
➤ **Give advice**

➤ **Ask for information at a hospital**
➤ **Describe healthy**
   and unhealthy practices

 LESSON 1

Parts of the body

GOAL ➤ **Identify parts of the body**

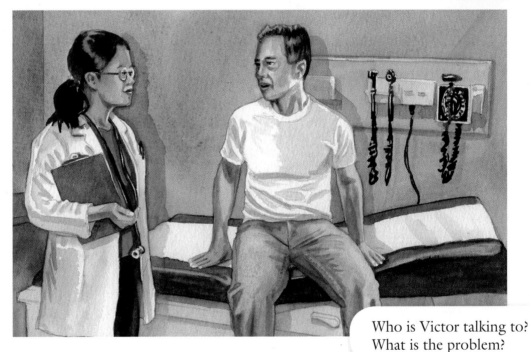

Who is Victor talking to?
What is the problem?

A Read about Victor.

Victor is sick. He needs to visit the doctor. The doctor asks, "What is the problem?" Victor answers, "My legs hurt, my chest hurts, and my back hurts." The doctor gives Victor some medicine.

B Circle *True* or *False*.

1. Victor needs medicine.   True   False

2. Victor's head hurts.   True   False

3. Victor doesn't have a problem.   True   False

GOAL ➤ **Identify parts of the body**

C Use the words from the boxes to label the pictures.

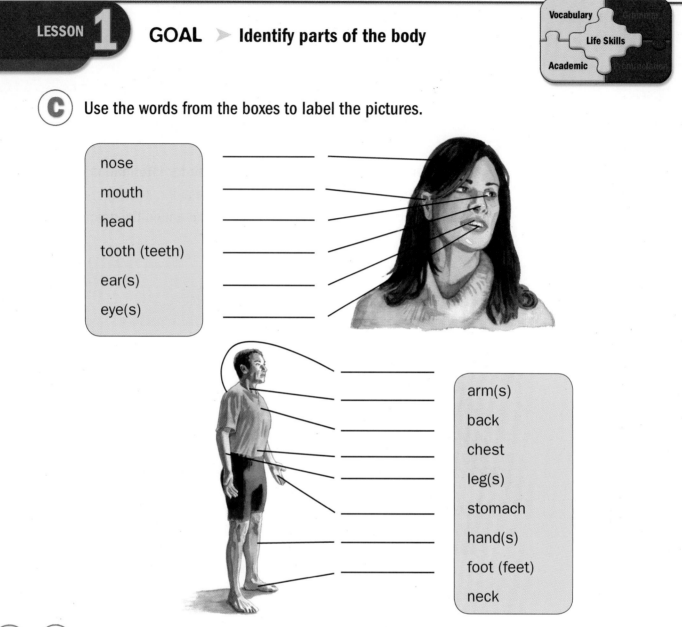

nose

mouth

head

tooth (teeth)

ear(s)

eye(s)

_____ _____

_____ _____

_____

_____

_____

_____

arm(s)

back

chest

leg(s)

stomach

hand(s)

foot (feet)

neck

_____

_____

_____

_____

_____

_____

CD 2
TR 12–14

D Listen to the patients talk to the doctor. What are their problems? Complete the sentences.

1. *Karen:*   Doctor, my _____ hurts.

2. *Roberto:*   Doctor, my _____ hurts.

3. *Tino:*   Doctor, my _____ and _____ hurt.

E Read the conversation. Practice new conversations using the words in Exercise C.

Doctor: What is the problem today?
Patient: My <u>leg hurts.</u>
Doctor: Your <u>leg</u>?
Patient: Yes, my <u>leg</u>.

F Study the chart with your classmates and teacher.

Simple Present		
Subject	**Verb**	**Example sentence**
it my leg my arm my foot my head	hurts	My leg **hurts.** My arm **hurts.** My head **hurts.**
they my legs my arms my feet my ears	hurt	My legs **hurt.** My feet **hurt.** My ears **hurt.**

G Write sentences for singular and plural subjects.

Part of body	Singular	Plural
leg	My leg hurts.	My legs hurt.
arm	My arm hurts.	My arms hurt.
head		
foot		
back		
eye		
nose		
ear		

H In groups, make a list of body parts from this lesson. Rank the body parts. Number 1 is the most important.

What's the problem?

GOAL ➤ Identify illnesses and health problems

Vocabulary
Life Skills
Academic Pronunciation

A Label the picture with the words from the box.

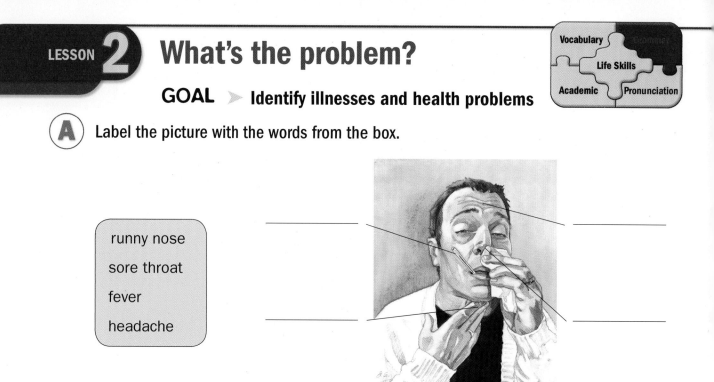

> runny nose
>
> sore throat
>
> fever
>
> headache

B Listen and practice the conversation.

CD 2
TR 15

Doctor: What's the matter?
Miguel: Doctor, I feel very sick. I have a terrible sore throat.
Doctor: You have the flu.
Miguel: The flu?
Doctor: Yes, the flu!

Pronunciation

Intonation: Information Questions

➤ What's the matter?

Intonation: Clarification Questions

➤ The flu?

C Listen to each conversation. Circle the problem.

CD 2
TR 16–19

1. sore throat	runny nose	fever	headache
2. sore throat	runny nose	fever	headache
3. sore throat	runny nose	fever	headache
4. sore throat	runny nose	fever	headache

GOAL ➤ **Identify illnesses and health problems**

D Read the chart with your classmates and teacher.

Common cold symptoms	Common flu symptoms
low fever	high fever
sore throat	sore throat
headache	headache
runny nose	muscle aches
	dry cough

E Complete the diagram using the information in Exercise D.

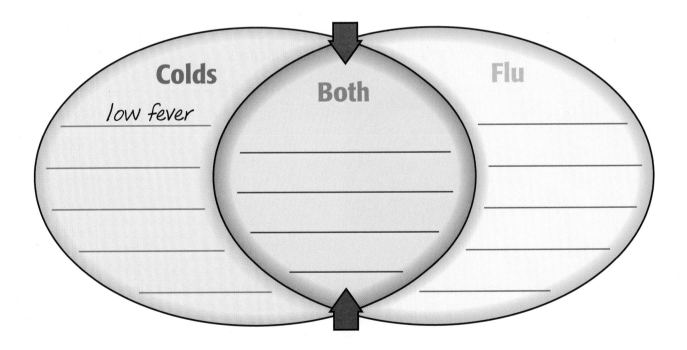

GOAL > **Identify illnesses and health problems**

F Study the charts with your classmates and teacher.

Simple Present: *Have*		
Subject	***Have***	**Example sentence**
I, you, we, they	have	I **have** a headache. You **have** a sore throat.
he, she, it	has	She **has** a stomachache. He **has** a fever.

Negative Simple Present: *Have*			
Subject	**Negative**	***Have***	**Example sentence**
I, you, we, they	do not (don't)	have	I **don't have** a headache. You **don't have** a sore throat.
he, she, it	does not (doesn't)	have	She **doesn't have** a stomachache. He **doesn't have** a fever.

G Read the symptoms and complete the sentences.

headache

stomachache

fever

1. Armando _____ a headache.

2. He _____ a cough.

3. He _____ a fever.

4. He _____ an earache.

5. He _____ a sore throat.

6. He _____ a stomachache.

H What other illnesses do you know? Use a dictionary and list illnesses and symptoms.

Illness	Symptom
measles	red spots

What should I do?

GOAL ➤ Give advice

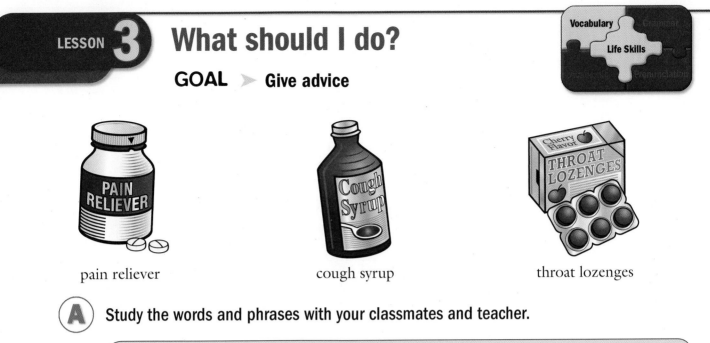

pain reliever   cough syrup   throat lozenges

A Study the words and phrases with your classmates and teacher.

rest	go to the doctor	take throat lozenges
take pain relievers	take cough syrup	

B What do you do when you have these symptoms? Complete the chart.

Symptom	Take pain relievers.	Rest.	Take cough syrup.	Take throat lozenges.	Go to the doctor.	Other
fever						
cough						
runny nose						
headache	✓					✓
sore throat						
stomachache						
backache						
feel tired						

C Practice the conversation. Then, use information from Exercise B to make more conversations.

Patient: I have a headache.
Doctor: Take pain relievers.
Patient: Thanks.

GOAL ➤ Give advice

What is Karen talking about?
What is the doctor writing?

D **Read about Karen.**

Karen is talking to the doctor. She is sick. Karen has a bad headache and sore throat. The doctor is giving Karen a prescription for some medicine. She needs to read the labels on the medicine carefully. The doctor is helping her understand them.

E **Read the statements. Circle *True* or *False*.**

1. Karen is sick. She has a backache.   True   False

2. The doctor doesn't give Karen medicine.   True   False

3. Karen should read the labels.   True   False

F **Read the labels.**

INSTRUCTIONS
Take two tablets
every three hours.

Take two
tablespoons
every four
hours.

Cherry
Flavor

Instructions
Take one lozenge
as needed for sore
throat pain.

Throat Lozenges

G **Listen to Karen reading the medicine labels. Write the medicine for each description.**

CD 2
TR 20

1. _____   2. _____   3. _____

GOAL ➤ Give advice

H Study the charts with your classmates and teacher.

Should			
Subject	*Should*	**Base verb**	**Example sentence**
I, you, he, she, it, we, they	should	rest	You **should** rest.
		stay	He **should** stay home.
		go	They **should** see a doctor.
		take	I **should** take pain relievers.
			We **should** take cough syrup.

Should (Negative)			
Subject	*Should*	**Base verb**	**Example sentence**
I, you, he, she, it, we, they	should not (shouldn't)	drive	You **shouldn't** drive and take this medicine.
		drink	He **shouldn't** drink alcohol with this medicine.
		go	We **shouldn't** go out.

I Read each problem and give advice. Use *should* and *shouldn't*.

1. Roberto has a cold.
   <u>He should take cold medicine and he shouldn't go out.</u>

2. Phuong and Nam have a cold.
   <u>They   .</u>

3. Michael has a sore throat.
   <u>He   .</u>

4. Ayumi has a fever.
   <u>She   .</u>

5. Oscar feels tired.
   <u>He   .</u>

6. Omar has a stomachache.
   <u>He   .</u>

J In a group, make a list of medications you have in your home.

There's an emergency!

GOAL ➤ Ask for information at a hospital

A Listen and practice the conversation.

CD 2
TR 21

Operator: What is the emergency?
Victor: There is a car accident.
Operator: Where is the accident?
Victor: It's on Fourth and Bush.
Operator: What is your name?
Victor: It's Victor Karaskov.
Operator: Is anyone hurt?
Victor: Yes. Please send an ambulance.

What is the problem?
What is Victor doing?

B Answer the questions.

1. Who is calling about the emergency?

   _____

2. What is the emergency?

   _____

3. Where is the emergency?

   _____

C With a partner, make a new conversation. Use one of the ideas in the chart below.

Who	What	Where
Antonio	A man is having a heart attack.	Broadway and Nutwood
Karen	There is a car accident.	First and Grand
Tran	A house is on fire.	234 Jones Avenue

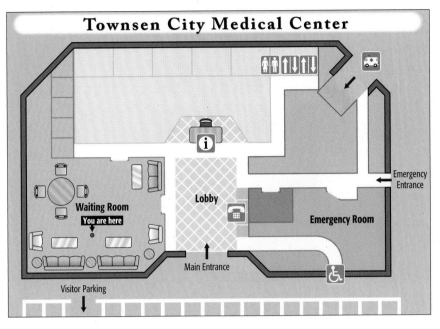

D Write the letters next to the correct symbols.

a. the wheelchair entrance   c. the elevators   e. the pay phones

b. the restrooms   d. Information   f. the ambulance entrance

1. ____

4. ____

2. ____

5. ____

3. ____

6. ____

> *is / are*
>
> Where **is** Information?
> **It is** here.
>
> Where **are** the restrooms?
> **They are** here.

E Ask questions about places on the directory.

EXAMPLES: *Student A:* Excuse me, where is Information?
                 Student B: It's here. (Student B points to the map.)

                 Student B: Excuse me, where are the elevators?
                 Student A: They are here. (Student A points to the map.)

  F **Listen to the conversations. Complete the sentences.**

CD 2
TR 22–25

1. The elevators are close to the _____ .

2. The wheelchair entrance is in the _____ .

3. The pay phones are close to the _____ .

4. Information is in the _____ .

G **Ask a partner for information. Ask about the elevators, the wheelchair entrance, the pay phones, and Information.**

EXAMPLE: *Student A:* Where are the restrooms?
Student B: They are close to the elevators.

H **In groups of four, prepare a role-play.**

Student 1: You work in Information.
Student 2: You are very sick.
Student 3: You are a family member.
Student 4: You are a nurse.

I **Active Task.** Visit the emergency room of a hospital. Find Information. Is there a directory?

Staying healthy

GOAL ➤ Describe healthy
and unhealthy practices

Vocabulary
Life Skills

Why is exercise important?

A Read about exercise.

We need to exercise. It is good for your heart, muscles, flexibility, and weight.
Everyone should exercise. People can run, swim, clean the house, or work in the yard.
Doctors say we should exercise every day.

B Match the words and the pictures.

_____ 1. muscles   _____ 2. weight   _____ 3. flexibility   _____ 4. heart

a.   b.   c.   d.

GOAL ➤ Describe healthy
and unhealthy practices

Vocabulary
Grammar
Life Skills
Academic
Pronunciation

C Study the bar graph with your classmates and teacher.

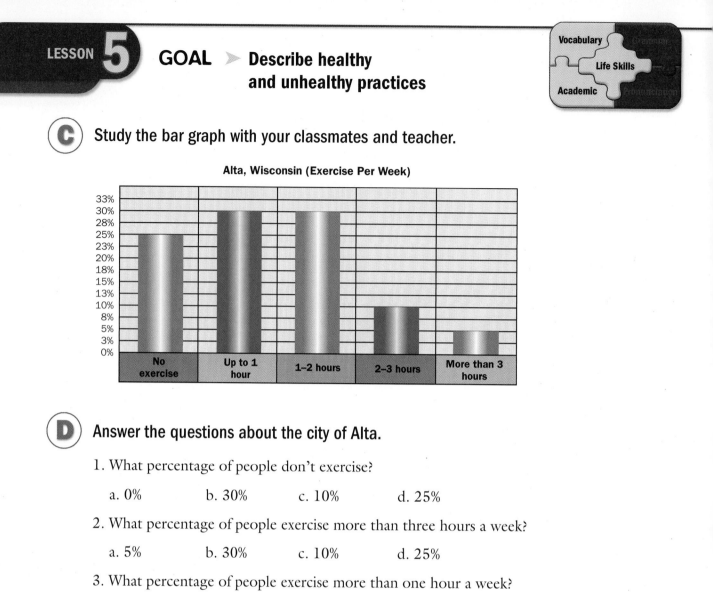

Alta, Wisconsin (Exercise Per Week)

D Answer the questions about the city of Alta.

1. What percentage of people don't exercise?

   a. 0%   b. 30%   c. 10%   d. 25%

2. What percentage of people exercise more than three hours a week?

   a. 5%   b. 30%   c. 10%   d. 25%

3. What percentage of people exercise more than one hour a week?

   a. 0%   b. 30%   c. 45%   d. 50%

E Listen to the conversations about exercise. Write the number under the correct picture.

CD 2
TR 26–29

a.   b.   c.   d.

_____   _____   _____   _____

GOAL ➤ Describe healthy
and unhealthy practices

 Study the chart with your classmates and teacher.

Infinitives			
Subject	**Verb**	**Infinitive (*to* + base)**	**Example sentence**
I, you, we, they	want	to run to exercise to walk	I want **to run.** We want **to exercise.** They want **to walk.**
he, she, it	wants	to ride to do to go	He wants **to ride** a bicycle. She wants **to do** yard work. She wants **to go** to the gym.

G Write three exercise goals. Use the ideas in Exercise F.

1. I want to _____ .

2. _____

3. _____

H Ask three classmates about their exercise goals. Write their goals.

1. He wants to _____ .

2. _____

3. _____

I Talk to four classmates. Complete the chart.

EXAMPLE: *Student A:* How much do you exercise every week?
　　　　　Student B: I exercise about one hour every week.

Amount of Exercise Per Week					
Name	**0 minutes**	**0–1 hour**	**1–2 hours**	**2–3 hours**	**more than 3 hours**

Review

A Look at the picture.
Write the words.
(Lesson 1)

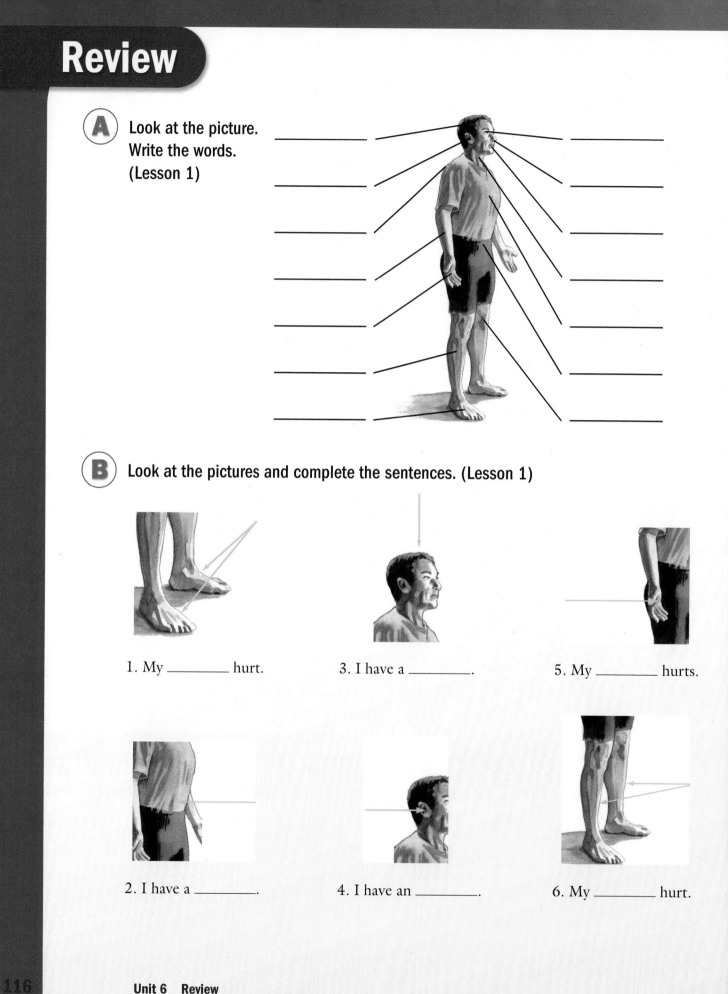

_____ _____

_____ _____

_____ _____

_____ _____

_____ _____

B Look at the pictures and complete the sentences. (Lesson 1)

1. My _____ hurt.

2. I have a _____.

3. I have a _____.

4. I have an _____.

5. My _____ hurts.

6. My _____ hurt.

C **Match the symptom and the remedy. (Lesson 3)**

_____ 1. fever   a. lozenges

_____ 2. feel tired   b. syrup

_____ 3. sore throat   c. rest

_____ 4. cough   d. pain reliever

D **Practice the conversation with a partner. Make similar conversations using the words in Exercise C. (Lessons 2 and 3)**

Student A: What's the matter?
Student B: I <u>have a headache</u>.
Student A: You should <u>take a pain reliever</u>.
Student B: Thanks. That's a good idea.

E **Read the medicine bottles and complete the chart. (Lesson 3)**

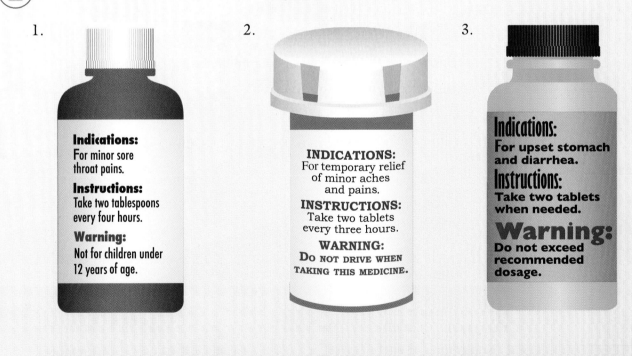

1.

Indications:
For minor sore throat pains.

Instructions:
Take two tablespoons every four hours.

Warning:
Not for children under 12 years of age.

2.

INDICATIONS:
For temporary relief of minor aches and pains.

INSTRUCTIONS:
Take two tablets every three hours.

WARNING:
DO NOT DRIVE WHEN TAKING THIS MEDICINE.

3.

Indications:
For upset stomach and diarrhea.

Instructions:
Take two tablets when needed.

Warning:
Do not exceed recommended dosage.

	How many?	How often?
1.	two tablespoons	every four hours
2.		
3.		

Review

F Complete the sentences with *should or shouldn't*. (Lesson 3)

should

shouldn't

1. He ___should___ take medicine.

2. We _____ rest.

3. They _____ go to the doctor.

4. We _____ exercise every day.

1. I _____ drink and drive.

2. He _____ take four tablets.

3. We _____ go out.

4. They _____ drive and take this medicine.

G Read the conversation and put the sentences in the correct order. (Lesson 4)

_____ *Victor:* There's a car accident.

___1___ *Operator:* 911, what is the emergency?

_____ *Victor:* Yes.

_____ *Victor:* It's on Fourth and Bush.

_____ *Operator:* Is anyone hurt?

_____ *Operator:* OK. The police and ambulance are on the way.

_____ *Operator:* Where is the accident?

H Write six items you can find in a hospital. (Lesson 4)

_____   _____   _____

_____   _____   _____

I Ask three classmates about their exercise goals. Complete the chart. (Lesson 5)

Name	What exercise do you want to do?	When do you want to do this exercise?	How long do you want to do this exercise?
Nadia	swim	8 A.M. on Saturdays	40 minutes

My Dictionary

Make flash cards to improve your vocabulary.

1. Choose four new words from this unit.

2. Write each word on an index card or on a sheet of paper.

3. On the back of the index card or paper, draw a picture, find and write a sentence from the book with the word, and write the page number.

4. Study the words.

My <u>arm</u> hurts.
page 103

Learner Log

Circle how well you learned each item and write the page number where you learned it.

1. I can identify body parts.

   Yes   Maybe   No   Page _____

2. I can identify symptoms.

   Yes   Maybe   No   Page _____

3. I can identify medicines and read labels.

   Yes   Maybe   No   Page _____

4. I can ask for and give information.

   Yes   Maybe   No   Page _____

5. I can describe healthy activities.

   Yes   Maybe   No   Page _____

Rank what you like to do best from 1 to 6. 1 is your favorite activity. Your teacher will help you.

_____ Practice listening

_____ Practice speaking

_____ Practice reading

_____ Practice writing

_____ Learn new words

_____ Learn grammar

In the next unit, I want to practice more

_____.

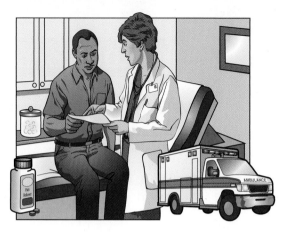

Create a role-play about an emergency.

In this project, you will create a role-play. Your group will perform the role-play for the class. Members of your group will take on the roles of a patient, a family member, a 911 operator, a doctor, and a worker at the hospital.

1. Form a team of four or five students. In your team, you need:

POSITION	JOB	STUDENT NAME
Student 1: **Team Leader**	See that everyone speaks English. See that everyone participates.	
Student 2: **Secretary**	Write out the role-play with help from the team. Make sure there is a part for everyone.	
Student 3: **Director**	Direct the role-play.	
Students 4/5: **Spokespeople**	Introduce the role-play.	

2. Choose an accident or illness. Write down the injured or sick person's symptoms. Who is the patient in your group? What is his or her name in the role-play?

3. Write a conversation with a 911 operator.

4. Write a conversation with a doctor. Write a medicine label with directions. In the conversation, the doctor gives a prescription.

5. Write a conversation with a family member of the patient.

6. Put the conversations together.

7. Present the role-play.

Working on It

GOALS

➤ Identify common occupations
➤ Interpret classified ads
➤ Write your job history
➤ Perform a job interview
➤ Interpret performance reviews

LESSON **1**

What's your job?

GOAL ➤ Identify common occupations

Vocabulary · Grammar · Life Skills · Academic · Pronunciation

A Write the jobs from the box under the pictures.

| teller | nurse | office worker | server | mechanic |

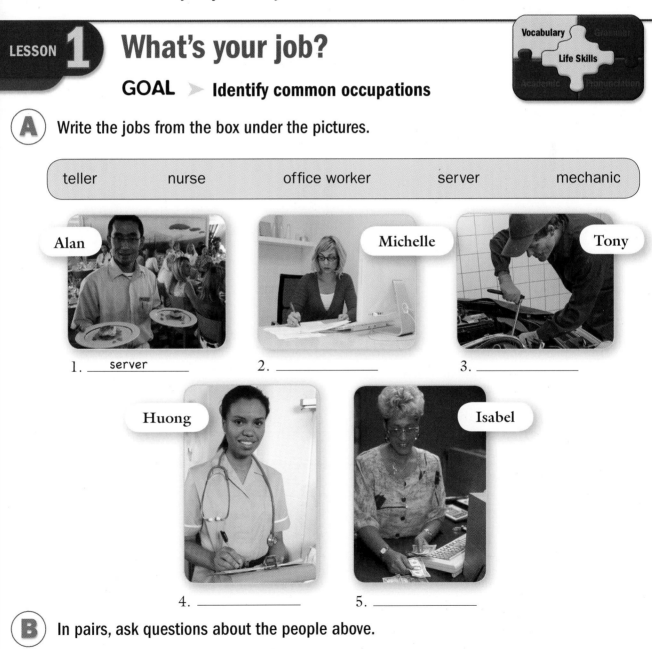

Alan

Michelle

Tony

1. <u>server</u>

2. <u>_____</u>

3. <u>_____</u>

Huong

Isabel

4. <u>_____</u>

5. <u>_____</u>

B In pairs, ask questions about the people above.

EXAMPLES:
Student A: What is Tony's job?
Student B: He is a mechanic.

Student B: What does Tony do?
Student A: He's a mechanic.

GOAL ➤ **Identify common occupations**

Vocabulary
Life Skills
Academic

C Study the pictures with your classmates and teacher.

1. cook/chef

3. server

5. custodian

2. cashier

4. secretary

6. teacher

D Write the job titles from Exercise C in the correct column.

Restaurant	School
cook / chef	secretary

E Listen to each conversation. Circle the correct job title.

CD 2
TR 30-33

1. secretary	teacher	custodian
2. cashier	server	cook
3. secretary	teacher	custodian
4. cashier	server	cook

F Study the charts with your classmates and teacher.

Simple Present		
Subject	**Verb**	**Example sentence**
I, you, we, they	work	I **work** in an office.
he, she, it	works	He **works** in a restaurant.

Negative Simple Present			
Subject	**Negative**	**Verb**	**Example sentence**
I, you, we, they	do not (don't)	work	I **don't work** in an office. You **don't work** in a restaurant.
he, she, it	does not (doesn't)		He **doesn't work** in a school. She **doesn't work** in a hospital.

G Look at the jobs in Exercise C. Ask and answer questions by pointing to each picture.

EXAMPLE: *Student A:* What does he do? (Point to the cook.)
Student B: He is a <u>cook</u>.
Student A: He works <u>in a school</u>, right?
Student B: No, he doesn't work <u>in a school</u>. He works <u>in a restaurant</u>.

Pronunciation

Emphasis
Put emphasis on requested information and on corrected information.

➤ He works IN A SCHOOL, right?

➤ No, he doesn't work IN A SCHOOL. He works IN A RESTAURANT.

H Talk to three classmates. Complete the chart. Then, report to a group.

EXAMPLE: Huong is a nurse. She works in a hospital.

Name	What do you do?	Where do you work?
Huong	nurse	hospital

Job hunting

GOAL ➤ Interpret classified ads

A Read the classified ad.

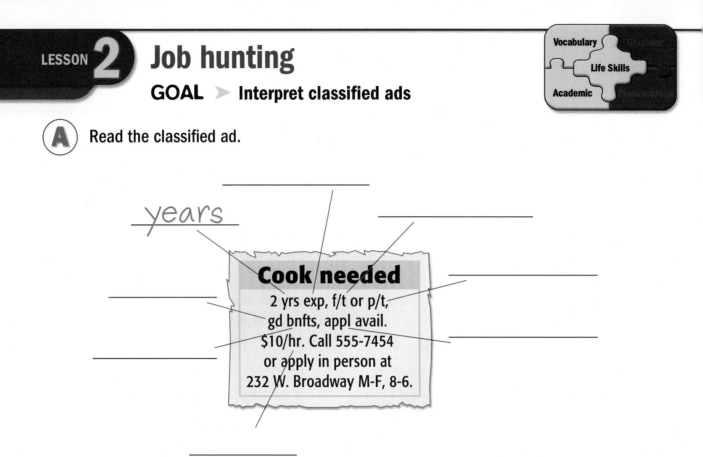

_____

years

_____

Cook needed
2 yrs exp, f/t or p/t,
gd bnfts, appl avail.
$10/hr. Call 555-7454
or apply in person at
232 W. Broadway M-F, 8-6.

_____

_____

_____

_____

_____

B Write the words from the box with the abbreviations above.

~~years~~	part-time	full-time	benefits
good	application	experience	hour

C Listen to the conversations. Bubble in the correct benefits.

CD 2
TR 34–36

1. Listen to Roberto and his boss. Bubble in the benefit.

   ○ vacation   ○ sick leave   ○ insurance

2. Listen to Anya and her supervisor. Bubble in the benefit.

   ○ vacation   ○ sick leave   ○ insurance

3. Listen to Steve and his manager. Bubble in the benefit.

   ○ vacation   ○ sick leave   ○ insurance

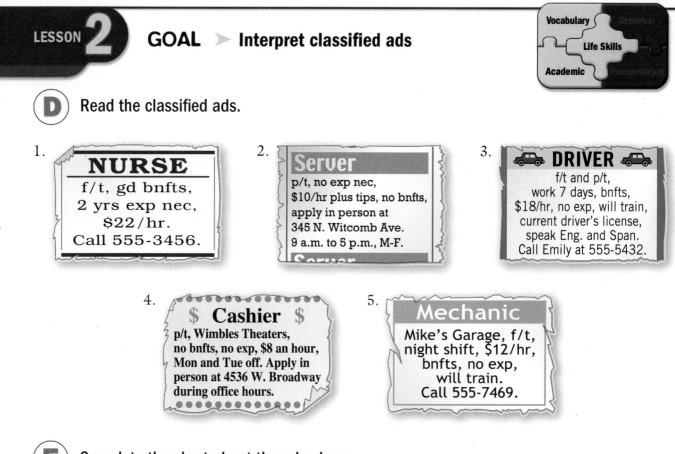

D Read the classified ads.

1.
NURSE
f/t, gd bnfts,
2 yrs exp nec,
$22/hr.
Call 555-3456.

2.
Server
p/t, no exp nec,
$10/hr plus tips, no bnfts,
apply in person at
345 N. Witcomb Ave.
9 a.m. to 5 p.m., M-F.
Server

3.
DRIVER
f/t and p/t,
work 7 days, bnfts,
$18/hr, no exp, will train,
current driver's license,
speak Eng. and Span.
Call Emily at 555-5432.

4.
$ Cashier $
p/t, Wimbles Theaters,
no bnfts, no exp, $8 an hour,
Mon and Tue off. Apply in
person at 4536 W. Broadway
during office hours.

5.
Mechanic
Mike's Garage, f/t,
night shift, $12/hr,
bnfts, no exp,
will train.
Call 555-7469.

E Complete the chart about the ads above.

Position	Experience	Full-time or Part-time	Benefits (Yes/No)	Pay
1.	2 years			
2. server				
3.		f/t or p/t		
4.			No	
5.				$12/hr

F Listen and write the missing words.

CD 2
TR 37

We need a _____ for our restaurant in San Francisco. The salary is

_____ an hour. You need _____ years experience

for this job. This is a full-time position with benefits. We offer _____

and a two-week _____ every year. Apply in person at 3500 West Arbor

Place, San Francisco, California.

GOAL ➤ Interpret classified ads

Life Skills

G Read about Silvia, Phuong, and Amal.

Silvia

Phuong

Amal

Skills:
She can drive.
She can speak English.
She can speak Spanish.
She can work at night.
Needs:
She needs a part-time job.

Skills:
She can't drive.
She can speak English.
She can't work at night.
She can't speak Spanish.
Needs:
She needs a part-time job.

Skills:
He can drive.
He can speak English.
He can't speak Spanish.
He can work at night.
Needs:
He needs a full-time job.

H Work in a group. Look at the classified ads in Exercise D. Write the jobs that are good for Silvia, Phuong, and Amal.

Silvia	Phuong	Amal

I In a group, write a classified ad. Look at Exercise D for help.

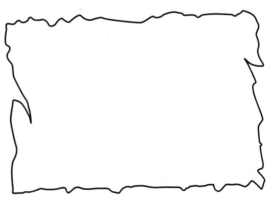

J **Active Task.** Look in the newspaper or on the Internet to find a job you want. Tell the class about the job.

What was your job before?

GOAL ➤ Write your job history

What is Francisco's job?
Does he work inside or outside?

 A **Read about Francisco.**

My name is Francisco. I'm from Guatemala. Now I work in the United States. I'm a mail carrier. I deliver mail to about two hundred houses every day. I started my job in July of 2005. Before I moved to the United States, I was a cook from March, 2000 to July 2005. I cooked hamburgers and french fries in a fast-food restaurant.

B **Answer the questions.**

1. Where is Francisco from? _____

2. What is his job now? _____

3. What does he do in his job? _____

4. When did he start his job? _____

5. What was his job in Guatemala? _____

6. Where did he work in Guatemala? _____

C **Complete the job history for Francisco.**

Job History

POSITION	COMPANY	FROM	TO	DUTIES (Responsibilities)
Mail carrier	US Government			
	Mr. Burger			
Busboy	La Cantina	March 1998	March 2000	cleaned tables

D Study the charts with your classmates and teacher.

Simple Past: Regular Verbs			
Subject	**Base verb + *ed***		**Example sentence**
I, you, he, she, it, we, they	cleaned	tables	I **cleaned** tables.
	cooked	hamburgers	You **cooked** hamburgers.
	prepared	breakfast	He **prepared** breakfast.
	delivered	packages	She **delivered** packages.
	counted	the money	It **counted** the money.
	helped	other workers	We **helped** other workers.
	moved	to the United States	They **moved** to the United States.

Simple Past: *Be*			
Subject	***Be***		**Example sentence**
I, he, she, it	was	a mail carrier	I **was** a mail carrier.
we, you, they	were	happy	You **were** happy.

E Complete each sentence with the correct form of the word in parentheses.

1. Anya was an office worker.

   She _____typed_____ (type) letters.

2. Ernesto was a delivery person.

   He _____ (deliver) packages.

3. David was a cashier.

   He _____ (count) money.

4. Anita was a nurse.

   She _____ (help) the doctors.

5. Eva and Anya were teachers.

   They _____ (work) in a school.

6. Derek was a salesperson.

   He _____ (talk) to customers.

7. So was a mechanic.

   He _____ (fix) cars.

8. Mary was a cook.

   She _____ (prepare) lunch.

9. Agatha was a manager.

   She _____ (supervise) the other workers.

10. I was a _____.

    I _____.

F Practice the conversation with your partner. Then, make new conversations using the information below.

Miyuki: What was your last job?
Anya: I was <u>an office worker</u>.
Miyuki: What did you do as <u>an office worker</u>?
Anya: I <u>typed letters</u>.
Miyuki: What do you do now?
Anya: I am <u>a student</u>. I <u>study English</u>.

Before	**After**
1. office worker / type letters	student / study English
2. teacher / help students	writer / write books
3. mechanic / fix cars	driver / drive a taxi
4. mail carrier / deliver letters	salesperson / sell computers
5. cook / cook hamburgers	server / serve food
6. busboy / clean tables	cashier / count money

CD 2
TR 38

G Listen and complete the job history. Then, practice the conversation in Exercise F again with the new information.

POSITION	COMPANY	FROM	TO	DUTIES (Responsibilities)
Nurse	Arch Memorial Hospital	February 2004	Present	
Office worker	Arch Memorial Hospital	May 2001	February 2004	
Receptionist	Arch Memorial Hospital	January 1998	May 2001	

H Look at the job history. Complete the job history for yourself.

POSITION	COMPANY	FROM	TO	DUTIES (Responsibilities)

I **Active Task.** Get a job application from a business or find one on the Internet. How much can you complete? Can you complete the job history section?

LESSON 4 A job interview

GOAL ➤ **Perform a job interview**

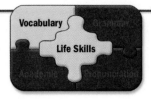

A Look at the pictures. What is good at a job interview? What is not good?

chewing gum

smoking

firm handshake

eye contact

good posture

bright clothing

B Use the words above to complete the chart. Then, add your own ideas.

Good at a job interview	Not good at a job interview
firm handshake	chewing gum

CD 2
TR 39–41

C Listen and complete the conversations with the words from the box.

> Thank you.
>
> I'm sorry. I can make an appointment.
>
> Who do I talk to for an appointment?

1. *Juan:* Excuse me. May I speak to you?
   Manager: Please make an appointment.
   Juan: _____

2. *Juan:* Excuse me. May I speak to you?
   Manager: Sure. Come in and sit down.
   Juan: _____

3. *Juan:* Excuse me. May I speak to you?
   Manager: Not right now. I'm busy.
   Juan: _____

 D Match each question with a clarification question. Draw lines.

1. What is your name?   a. Experience for this job?

2. What do you do?   b. My name?

3. Do you have experience?   c. Full-time?

4. Can you work eight hours?   d. On the weekends?

5. Can you work on Saturdays?   e. What is my job now?

Pronunciation

Intonation: *Clarification Questions*

➤ My name?

➤ On the weekends?

Who is Miyuki talking to?
What is she doing?

E Read the questions. Talk about them with your classmates and teacher.

Can I have an application?	Can I see the manager?
Can I make an appointment, please?	Can I show you my resume?

F Complete the conversations with the questions in the box above.

1. *Miyuki:* Excuse me. I'm interested in a job. Do you have any openings?
   Manager: Not right now, but we will keep your name on file if you fill out an application.
   Miyuki: _____

2. *Miyuki:* Here is my application. Can I see a manager?
   Office Worker: Not right now. She is busy.
   Miyuki: _____

3. *Manager:* Are you interested in the job as a clerk?
   Miyuki: Yes, that's right.
   Manager: Do you have any experience?
   Miyuki: _____

4. *Miyuki:* I am here for my interview. _____
   Office Worker: What time is your appointment?
   Miyuki: It's at 3:00 P.M.

G What personal information do you need to give in an interview? Make a list with a group.

name	

H Prepare a practice interview with a partner. Use the information from this lesson to help you.

He's a good worker.

GOAL ➤ Interpret performance reviews

A Look at Fernando's evaluation. What is good? What is a problem?

Evaluation Form

DATE: May 4, 2008
COMPANY: Paul's Radio and CD
NAME: Fernando Gaspar
POSITION: Sales Clerk
SUPERVISOR: Leticia Garcia

Punctuality:
Superior   Good   (Needs improvement)

Appearance (professional dress and grooming):
(Superior)   Good   Needs improvement

Communication Skills:
Superior   (Good)   Needs improvement

Product Knowledge:
Superior   (Good)   Needs improvement

Fernando is a good employee. I worked with him for eight hours today. He talked with the customers well. He was ten minutes late to work. This is a problem. He said he had a problem with his car. Fernando is a good salesperson and he has very good knowledge of the product.

SIGNED: *Leticia Garcia*

B Look at the evaluation and answer the questions.

1. Where does Fernando work? _____

2. What is his supervisor's name? _____

3. What does Fernando do well? _____

4. What does he do very well? _____

5. What does he need to improve? _____

C Study the charts with your classmates and teacher.

Simple Present: *Be*			
Subject	**Be**		**Example sentence**
I	am		I **am** always early.
he, she, it	is	early late on time punctual	He **is** sometimes late. She **is** a good worker.
we, you, they	are		We **are** often early. You **are** never on time. They **are** always punctual.

Adverbs of Frequency

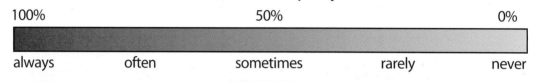

100%		50%		0%
always	often	sometimes	rarely	never

Simple Past: *Be*			
Subject	**Be**		**Example sentence**
I, he, she, it	was	early late on time punctual	I **was** early yesterday. He **was** often late. She **was** always a good worker.
we, you, they	were		We **were** early on Saturday. You **were** on time today. They **were** never punctual.

D Complete the sentences with the correct form of *be*.

1. Mario and Alberto _____were_____ early to work yesterday.

2. I _____ never on time last year, but now I _____ always on time.

3. She _____ punctual every day last year.

4. We come to work on time every day. We _____ rarely late.

5. You _____ a good worker. You always work well with customers.

E Read about Alberto. Underline the *be* verbs.

Alberto is a good worker. He works at night. He is punctual. The customers love him. Last night, Alberto was late for work. He had a problem with his car. His car is old. He called a tow truck with his cell phone and the tow truck was late.

GOAL ➤ **Interpret performance reviews**

CD 2
TR 42

F Listen to John's evaluation. Circle the correct rating *(needs improvement, good,* or *superior).*

EVALUATION FORM

DATE: May 4, 2008
COMPANY: Paul's Radio and CD
NAME: John Perkins
POSITION: Sales Clerk
SUPERVISOR: Leticia Garcia

Punctuality:

| Superior | Good | Needs improvement |

Appearance (professional dress and grooming):

| Superior | Good | Needs improvement |

Communication Skills:

| Superior | Good | Needs improvement |

Product Knowledge:

| Superior | Good | Needs improvement |

Comments:

I worked with John for four hours. He is new. He needs to learn more about the product. He doesn't dress well and he needs to comb his hair. He said he was tired today. I think he has three jobs. This is a problem. John communicates well with the customers.

Signed: *Leticia Garcia*

G In a group, rank the areas 1–4. Number 1 is the most important.

_____ Punctuality

_____ Appearance

_____ Communication

_____ Product Knowledge

Review

A Write the name of the job below each picture. (Lesson 1)

1._____

2._____

3._____

B Read the ads and complete the chart below. (Lesson 2)

1.
★ **Office** ★
Assistant

f/t, gd bnfts,
4 yrs exp nec,
$17/hr,
Call 555-2298.

2.
Restaurant Manager

p/t, restaurant exp nec,
$14/hr, no bnfts,
Apply in person
at 2222 E. Fourth St.
8am to 12pm, M-F.

3.
**Delivery
Person**

p/t, work 7 days, no bnfts,
$8/hr, no exp, will train,
current driver's license,
speak Eng. and Span.
Call 555-5477.

4.
CARPENTER

f/t, good bnfts, no exp,
$22 an hour,
must be 18 yrs. old.
Apply in person at
3333 W. Broadway
during office hours.

5.
Mechanic

Mike's Garage
f/t, night shift,
$12/hour, no exp nec,
will train, bnfts,
Call 555-7469.

Position	Experience	F/T or P/T	Benefits	Pay
1.				
2.				
3.				
4.				
5.				

C Write a classified ad for a receptionist. (Lesson 2)

_____

_____

_____

_____

_____

 D Complete the paragraph with the past tense form of the verbs in parentheses. (Lesson 3)

In 1995, Jarek was a carpenter. He _____ (construct) homes for Builders Plus Company. In 1997, Jarek was a custodian. He _____ (clean) the offices for Clean Sweep Maintenance Company. In 2000, Jarek was a server. He _____ (talk) to customers at the Polish Café. Now Jarek is a teacher. He helps students at Jefferson Adult School.

 E Complete the job history for Jarek. (Lesson 3).

POSITION	COMPANY	FROM	TO	DUTIES (Responsibilities)

Review

F Label the pictures and circle *good* or *bad* for a job interview. (Lesson 4)

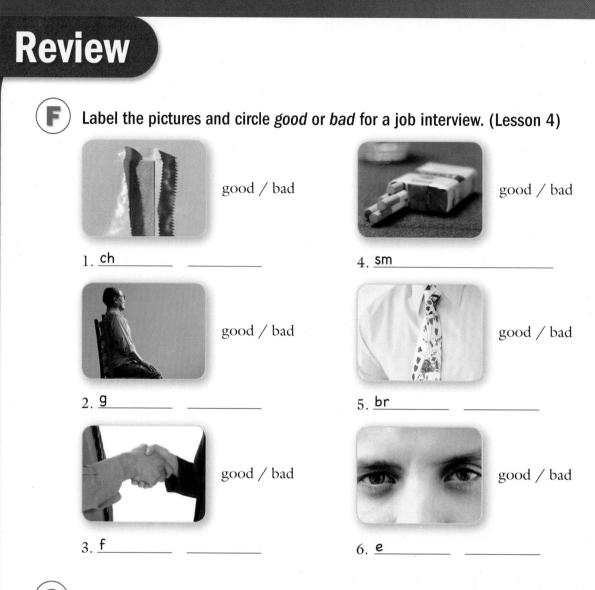

1. ch _____ _____   good / bad

2. g _____ _____   good / bad

3. f _____ _____   good / bad

4. sm _____   good / bad

5. br _____ _____   good / bad

6. e _____ _____   good / bad

G Complete the paragraph with the correct form of the verbs from the box. Choose the present or past tense. You will use one of the verbs two times. (Lessons 3 and 5)

be	move	work	live	help	deliver	like

Francisco _____ in Guatemala before he _____ to California. In Guatemala, he _____ a cook at a small fast-food restaurant. He _____ in the kitchen. He _____ 14 hours every day. Now he _____ a mail carrier in California. He _____ letters and packages. He _____ his new job very much.

H Match the words and definitions. Draw lines. (Lesson 5)

1. punctuality   a. clothing and posture

2. communicate   b. on time

3. appearance   c. talk

My Dictionary

Make flash cards to improve your vocabulary.

1. Choose four new words from this unit.

2. Write each word on an index card or on a sheet of paper.

3. On the back of the card or paper, draw a picture, find and write a sentence from the book with the word, and write the page number.

4. Study the words.

She delivered <u>packages.</u>
page 128

Learner Log

Circle how well you learned each item and write the page number where you learned it.

1. I can identify occupations.

   Yes   Maybe   No   Page _____

2. I can read classified ads.

   Yes   Maybe   No   Page _____

3. I can write my job history.

   Yes   Maybe   No   Page _____

4. I can ask good questions at a job interview.

   Yes   Maybe   No   Page _____

5. I can read a job evaluation.

   Yes   Maybe   No   Page _____

Rank what you like to do best from 1 to 6. 1 is your favorite activity. Your teacher will help you.

_____ Practice listening

_____ Practice speaking

_____ Practice reading

_____ Practice writing

_____ Learn new words

_____ Learn grammar

In the next unit, I want to practice more

_____.

Team Project

Get a new job.

In this project, you will prepare one member of your team to complete the process for getting a job.

1. Form a team with four or five students. In your team, you need:

POSITION	JOB	STUDENT NAME
Student 1: **Team Leader**	See that everyone speaks English. See that everyone participates.	
Student 2: **Writer**	With help from the team, write a classified ad, a job history, and a job evaluation.	
Student 3: **Director**	With help from the team, write and direct an interview.	
Students 4/5: **Spokespeople**	With help from the team, organize a presentation to give to the class.	

2. Choose one member of your team to look for a new job. Decide on a position he or she is interested in.

3. Write a classified ad describing the position.

4. Write a real or imaginary job history for the person looking for a job.

5. Write an imaginary job evaluation from an old job.

6. Write a conversation of a job interview and practice the conversation.

7. As a team, make a presentation of all the previous steps and perform the conversation.

UNIT 8

People and Learning

GOALS

➤ **Evaluate study habits**
➤ **Organize study**
➤ **Identify learning opportunities**

➤ **Identify work preferences**
➤ **Develop goals**

LESSON 1

How are your study habits?

GOAL ➤ **Evaluate study habits**

What is Nubar doing? Why?

A Read about Nubar.

Nubar is a good ESL student at Franklin Adult School. He comes to school every day. He also studies at home. Some students practice English at work. Others practice English with their families. Nubar learns two or three new words a day at home. Sometimes Nubar watches TV or listens to the radio.

B With a group, list ways to study English.

_____   _____

_____   _____

_____   _____

_____   _____

GOAL ➤ **Evaluate study habits**

C Study the charts with your classmates and teacher.

Regular Past Tense Verbs	
Base	**Simple past**
study	studied
participate	participated
help	helped
listen	listened
watch	watched
practice	practiced
learn	learned

Irregular Past Tense Verbs	
Base	**Simple past**
come	came
see	saw
write	wrote
speak	spoke
read	read
teach	taught

D Rewrite the sentences in the past tense.

1. Nubar comes to class every day.

   Nubar came to class every day.

2. Nubar studies at home.

   _____

3. Some students practice at work.

   _____

4. Some students watch TV or listen to the radio.

   _____

5. Nubar reads for one or two hours a day at home.

   _____

E Listen to Angela talk about her study skills. Check (✔) the things she did to study.

CD 2
TR 43

- ❏ came to class every day
- ❏ came to class on time
- ❏ helped other students
- ❏ learned new words every day
- ❏ listened to the radio

- ❏ participated in class
- ❏ practiced at work
- ❏ studied at home
- ❏ taught other students
- ❏ watched TV

F   Answer the questions about this course. Bubble in the correct answer.

Study Habits Questionnaire

1. How often did you come to class?
  ○ a. most of the time   ○ b. more than 50%   ○ c. less than 50%

2. Did you come to class on time?
  ○ a. most of the time   ○ b. more than 50%   ○ c. less than 50%

3. How much did you study at home each week?
  ○ a. more than 10 hours   ○ b. 5-10 hours   ○ c. less than 5 hours

4. Did you speak English in class and participate?
  ○ a. most of the time   ○ b. more than 50%   ○ c. less than 50%

5. Did you teach and help other students in class?
  ○ a. a lot   ○ b. a little   ○ c. never

6. Did you listen to the radio in English?
  ○ a. a lot   ○ b. a little   ○ c. never

7. Did you watch TV in English?
  ○ a. a lot   ○ b. a little   ○ c. never

8. Did you ask the teacher or other students questions when you didn't understand?
  ○ a. a lot   ○ b. a little   ○ c. never

How many *a* answers, *b* answers, and *c* answers do you have?

# of *a* answers _____	# of *b* answers _____	# of *c* answers _____

Do the math below.

of *a* answers x 3 = _____
of *b* answers x 2 = _____
of *c* answers x 1 = _____
    Total = _____

Score: **20-24** Super – You have great study habits!

Score: **16-19** Good – You have good study habits.

Score: **Under 16** – You need to change your study habits.

Staying organized

GOAL ➤ **Organize study**

Vocabulary · Grammar · Life Skills · Academic · Pronunciation

A Talk about the pictures with your classmates and teacher.

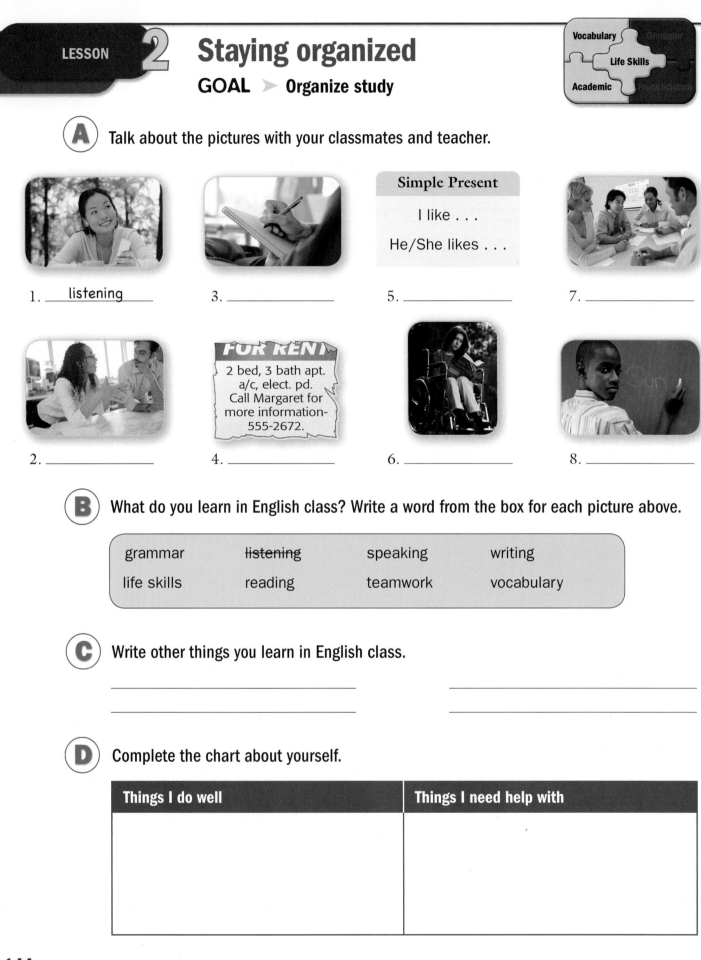

1. ___listening___

3. _____

Simple Present

I like . . .

He/She likes . . .

5. _____

7. _____

2. _____

FOR RENT

2 bed, 3 bath apt. a/c, elect. pd. Call Margaret for more information– 555-2672.

4. _____

6. _____

8. _____

B What do you learn in English class? Write a word from the box for each picture above.

grammar	~~listening~~	speaking	writing
life skills	reading	teamwork	vocabulary

C Write other things you learn in English class.

_____   _____

_____   _____

D Complete the chart about yourself.

Things I do well	Things I need help with

GOAL ➤ Organize study

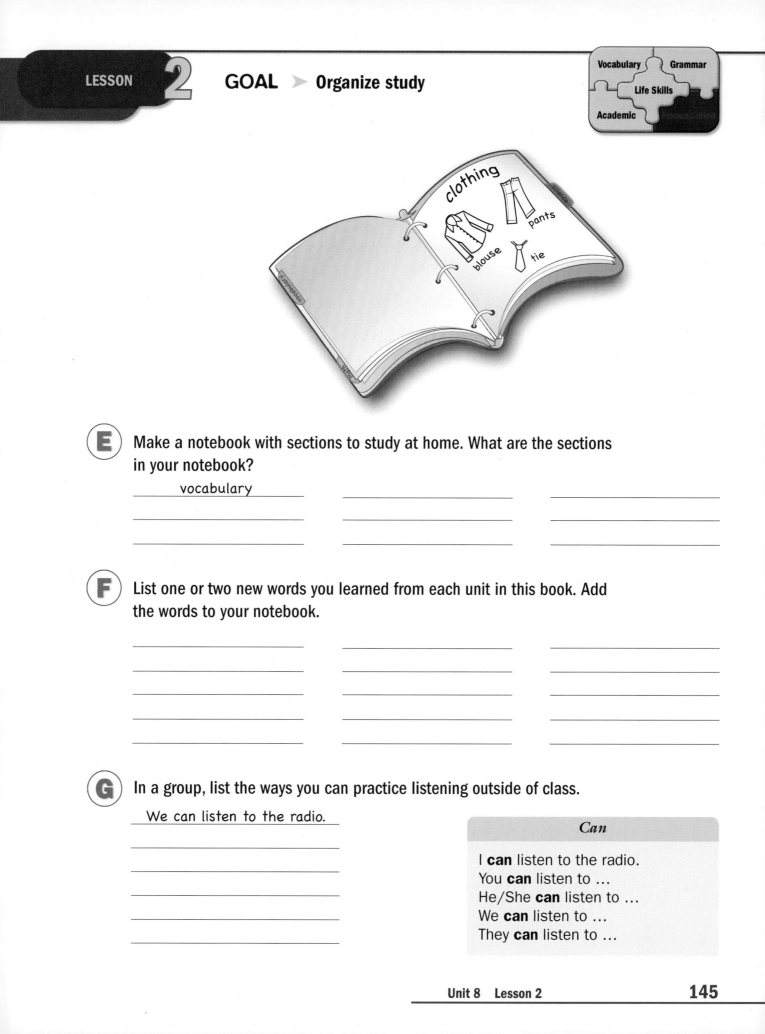

E Make a notebook with sections to study at home. What are the sections in your notebook?

___vocabulary___ _____ _____

_____ _____ _____

_____ _____ _____

F List one or two new words you learned from each unit in this book. Add the words to your notebook.

_____ _____ _____

_____ _____ _____

_____ _____ _____

_____ _____ _____

_____ _____ _____

G In a group, list the ways you can practice listening outside of class.

___We can listen to the radio.___

_____

_____

_____

_____

Can
I **can** listen to the radio.
You **can** listen to …
He/She **can** listen to …
We **can** listen to …
They **can** listen to …

H What are life skills? Read the paragraph.

Life skills are activities we often do every day. They include cooking, driving, and making appointments. Many students take the bus to school. They read bus schedules. Reading a bus schedule is a life skill. Asking questions and making appointments are also life skills. Every lesson in this book teaches a life skill.

CD 2
TR 44

I Listen and write the life skills you hear in the conversation. Write them here and in your notebook.

_____   _____

_____   _____

J Read the journal notes.

> *New Words: checkout, counter, cough*
> *Skill: I practiced in the supermarket. "Where is the medicine?"*
> *Book: I reviewed pages 10-15 in the textbook from last semester.*
> *Listening: TV—I watched Channel 20 for ten minutes at 7 A.M.*
> *Writing: I wrote in my journal.*

 K What did you do today to help you practice English?

Schools in the United States

GOAL ➤ **Identify learning opportunities**

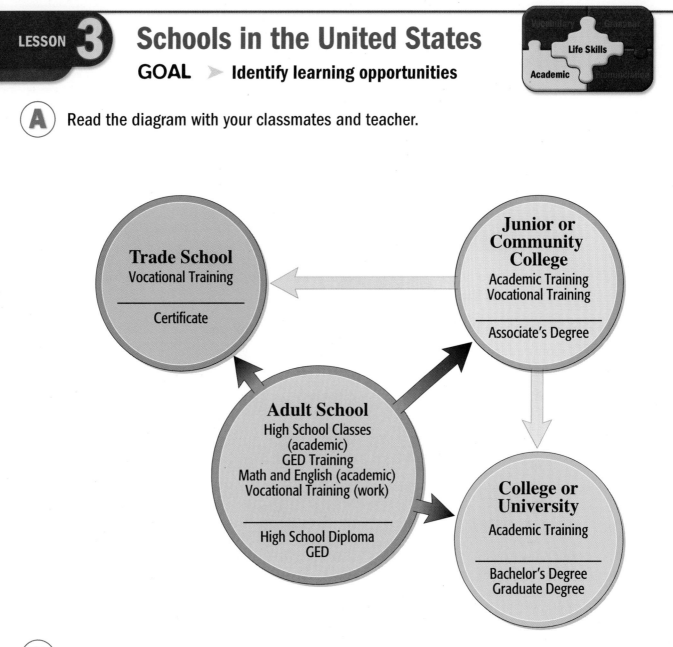

Life Skills
Academic

A Read the diagram with your classmates and teacher.

B Complete the chart about learning opportunities.

School	Degree or Diploma
Adult School	
Trade School	
Junior or Community College	
College or University	

C Read the information about the students. What kind of education do you think they need?

1.

Ahmed wants to be a computer technician.

❑ High School Diploma
❑ Community College
❑ University
❑ Trade School

3.

Minh wants to be a teacher.

❑ High School Diploma
❑ Community College
❑ University
❑ Trade School

5.

Mario wants to be a mechanic.

❑ High School Diploma
❑ Community College
❑ University
❑ Trade School

2.

Akiko wants to be a Web designer.

❑ High School Diploma
❑ Community College
❑ University
❑ Trade School

4.

Alan wants to be a cook.

❑ High School Diploma
❑ Community College
❑ University
❑ Trade School

6.

Marie wants to be a nurse's assistant.

❑ High School Diploma
❑ Community College
❑ University
❑ Trade School

D Listen to the conversations and check the correct information in Exercise C.

CD 2
TR 45–50

E Practice the conversation with a partner. Ask about the students in Exercise C.

Student A: Where should Ahmed go to school after the adult school?
Student B: He should go to a trade school.

Should
I **should** go to college. You **should** go … He/She **should** go … We **should** go … They **should** go …

GOAL ➤ Identify learning opportunities

Life Skills
Academic

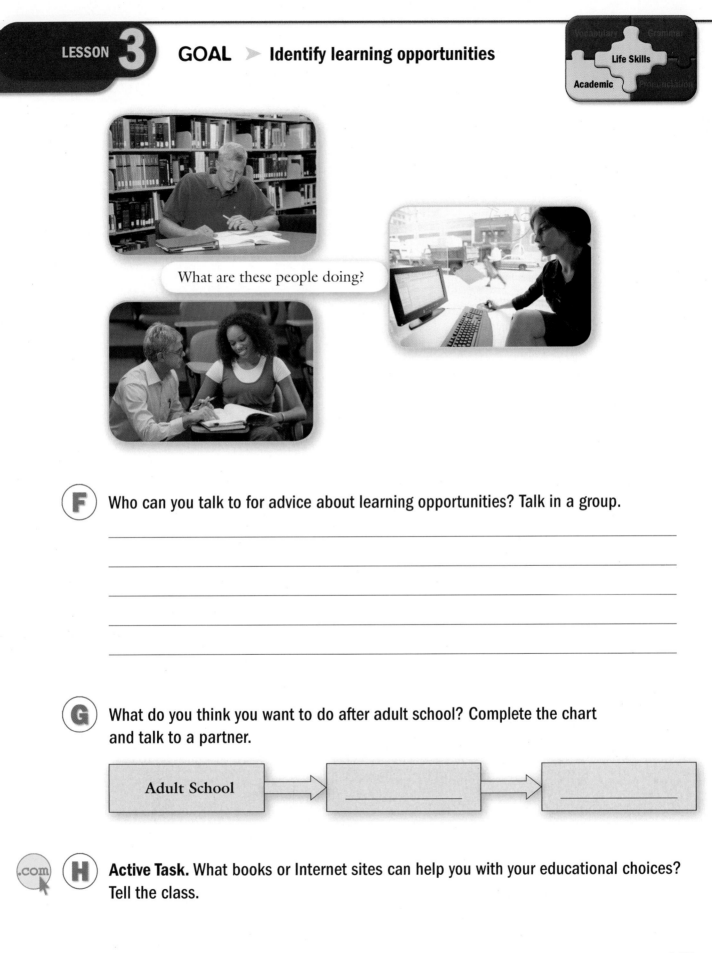

What are these people doing?

F Who can you talk to for advice about learning opportunities? Talk in a group.

_____

_____

_____

_____

_____

G What do you think you want to do after adult school? Complete the chart and talk to a partner.

| Adult School | ➡ | _____ | ➡ | _____ |

H **Active Task.** What books or Internet sites can help you with your educational choices? Tell the class.

Choosing the right job

GOAL ➤ Identify work preferences

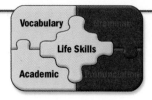

Vocabulary · Grammar · Life Skills · Academic · Pronunciation

A Read the information about the students. Circle the job that you think is the best for each one.

Position	Job
1. Roberto likes to study. He likes school. He likes history.	teacher mechanic doctor
2. Eva likes to help people. She likes to talk to people. She likes to study.	gardener nurse receptionist
3. Duong likes to work with his hands. He likes to fix things. He likes cars.	mechanic manager salesperson

B Listen to the conversations. Check Exercise A.

CD 2
TR 51–53

C Talk to a partner. List three things your partner likes to do.

_____ _____ _____

GOAL ➤ **Identify work preferences**

D Study the charts with your classmates and teacher.

Verb + Infinitive			
Subject	Verb	Infinitive	Example sentence
I, you, we, they	like want need	to read to travel to work to talk to handle to study	I like **to read**. You want **to travel**. We need **to work** alone. They like **to talk** on the phone.
he, she, it	likes wants needs		He likes **to handle** money. She wants **to study**.

Verb + Noun			
Subject	Verb	Noun	Example sentence
I, you, we, they	like want need	cars computer books school food	I like **cars**. You want a **computer**. We need **books**. They like **school**.
he, she, it	likes wants needs		He likes **computers**. She wants **food**.

E Complete each sentence with the correct form of the verb in parentheses.

1. They like _____ (work) outside.

2. He wants _____ (study) at school every day.

3. She needs _____ (make) money right now.

4. They want _____ (handle) money.

5. I want _____ (learn) English.

6. We like _____ (read) books.

7. I like _____ (talk) on the telephone.

8. You want _____ (work) at the university.

F Talk to a different partner than in Exercise C. List three things your partner likes. Report to a group.

_____   _____   _____

GOAL ➤ **Identify work preferences**

G A counselor is going to ask you questions to help you with your future plans. Answer the questions about yourself. Bubble in *Yes* or *No*.

PERSONAL INVENTORY

	Yes	No
1. Do you have a high school diploma?	◯	◯
2. Do you have good study skills?	◯	◯
3. Do you have experience?	◯	◯
4. Do you like technology (computers, machines)?	◯	◯
5. Do you like to do the same thing every day?	◯	◯
6. Do you like to handle money?	◯	◯
7. Do you like to read?	◯	◯
8. Do you like to study and to learn new things?	◯	◯
9. Do you like to listen to people?	◯	◯
10. Do you like to talk on the phone?	◯	◯
11. Do you like to travel?	◯	◯
12. Do you like to work with other people?	◯	◯
13. Do you like to work alone?	◯	◯
14. Do you like to work at night?	◯	◯
15. Do you like to work in the daytime?	◯	◯
16. Do you like to work with your hands?	◯	◯
17. Do you like your job?	◯	◯
18. Do you work now?	◯	◯
19. Do you have goals for the future?	◯	◯

H Discuss your answers in a group.

Making goals

GOAL ➤ Develop goals

A Read Nubar's journal entry. Answer the questions about his study goals.

September 5

    I have many study goals for the next month. I am going to read the

newspaper, listen to the radio, and talk to people in English every day.

I am also going to study four pages from my textbook every night

for 30 minutes in my bedroom.

---

1. When is Nubar going to study? _____

2. Where is Nubar going to study? _____

3. What is he going to study? _____

4. How long is he going to study? _____

CD 2
TR 54

B Look at the clocks. Then, listen to Nubar talk about his plans. Write what he is going to do next to the clocks. Use the phrases from the box.

> listen to the radio   read the newspaper   write in a journal
>
> review vocabulary   study the textbook

From [clock] to [clock] _____

From [clock] to [clock] _____

From [clock] to [clock] _____

C   Study the chart with your classmates and teacher.

Future with *Going to*			
Subject	*Going to*	**Base verb**	**Example sentence**
I	am going to (I'm going to)	learn	I **am going to** learn English.
you, we, they	are going to (you're/we're/they're going to)	listen practice read	We **are going to** practice English.
he, she, it	is going to (he's/she's going to)	speak study write	She **is going to** speak English.

D   Write sentences about Nubar's plans. Use the information from Exercise B.

1. <u>He is going to listen to the radio from 6:30 to 6:45 P.M.</u>

2. _____

3. _____

4. _____

E   What are your study plans? Write sentences and share them with a group.

1. <u>I</u> _____

2. _____

3. _____

4. _____

GOAL ➤ Develop goals

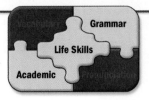

F Study another way to talk about future plans.

Future with *Will*			
Subject	***Will***	**Base**	**Example sentence**
I, you, he, she, it we, they	will	study work get married	I **will** study every day. She **will** work hard. They **will** get married.

G Read about Nubar's long-term goals.

> June 12
>
>   I have many goals for the future. Some of my goals will take a long time. I will study every day and get a high school diploma. After that, I will start college. I want to start in about three years. I also want to get married and have children sometime in the future. I will be a computer technician one day.

 H Nubar wants to do many things. Write his goals in the chart.

Family goals	Educational goals	Work goals
He wants to get married.		

I What are your family, educational, and work goals? Write them in the chart.

Family goals	Educational goals	Work goals

Review

A What are six things you did in this course to help you study English? Use the verbs from the box. Write sentences in the simple past tense. (Lesson 1)

> participate   help   speak   ask   read   listen   ~~come~~

EXAMPLE: I came to class on time. _____

1. _____

2. _____

3. _____

4. _____

5. _____

6. _____

B Bubble in the study skills. (Lesson 2)

○ learn English   ○ get a high school   ○ read
○ go to college   diploma   ○ write vocabulary
○ go to the   ○ listen carefully   words
   supermarket   ○ ask questions   ○ eat a good breakfast

C Write the things you can do well in class. (Lessons 1 and 2)

1. I can _____.

2. _____

3. _____

D Ask a partner: *What can you do well in class?* (Lessons 1 and 2)

EXAMPLE: He can listen well. OR She can ask questions well. _____

1. _____

2. _____

3. _____

E Complete the paragraph with the words from the box. (Lesson 3)

| degree | college | trade | diploma | GED | adult | certificate |

In the United States, adults can go to school in many different places. They can go to an _____ school to learn English or to get a high school _____ or _____. After adult school, students can study at a _____ or a _____ school. Students who go to a trade school get a _____ when they complete the courses. Some students get a _____ from a university after adult school.

F Complete the sentences with the correct form of the verb in parentheses. (Lesson 4)

1. Javier likes _____ (study) in the afternoon.

2. The students _____ (want) to learn English.

3. I _____ (like) books.

4. She _____ (like) to read books.

5. We want _____ (go) to college.

6. You need _____ (speak) to a teacher.

7. Eva _____ (want) to see the homework.

8. He likes _____ (work) at night.

Review

Nam

Now: Alton Adult School
Educational Goals: learn English,
    go to junior college
Work Goal: become a chef
Family Goal: buy a house

Gabriela

Now: Alton Adult School
Educational Goals: get a high school
    diploma, go to a trade school
Work Goal: become a nurse
Family Goal: get married

G Write sentences about Nam's future goals. Use *be going to.* (Lesson 5)

1. _____
2. _____
3. _____
4. _____

H Write sentences about Gabriela's future goals. Use *will.* (Lesson 5)

1. _____
2. _____
3. _____
4. _____

My Dictionary

Make flash cards to improve your vocabulary.

1. Choose four new words from this unit.

2. Write each word on an index card or on a sheet of paper.

3. On the back of the index card or paper, draw a picture, find and write a sentence from the book with the word, and write the page number.

4. Study the words.

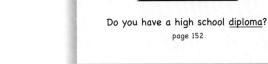

Do you have a high school <u>diploma</u>?
page 152

Learner Log

Circle how well you learned each item and write the page number where you learned it.

1. I can evaluate my study habits.

   Yes   Maybe   No   Page _____

2. I can identify study skills.

   Yes   Maybe   No   Page _____

3. I can identify learning opportunities.

   Yes   Maybe   No   Page _____

4. I can identify work preferences.

   Yes   Maybe   No   Page _____

5. I can develop goals.

   Yes   Maybe   No   Page _____

Rank what you like to do best from 1 to 6. 1 is your favorite activity. Your teacher will help you.

_____ Practice listening

_____ Practice speaking

_____ Practice reading

_____ Practice writing

_____ Learn new words

_____ Learn grammar

I think I improved most in

_____.

Team Project

Meet your goals.

In this project, you will plan your study time on a calendar. You will also write out your goals and plans in two paragraphs. You will work with a team, and your team will help you polish your paragraphs and calendar. Then, you will present your paragraphs and calendar to the class.

1. Complete a calendar for this month and next month. Write what days and what times you are going to do the following activities:

   - study your textbook
   - listen to the radio
   - read the newspaper
   - watch TV
   - review flash cards
   - write in your journal

2. Discuss your plans with your team.

3. Write a paragraph about your goals on another piece of paper. Start your paragraph like this:

   > I have many goals. I'm going to be able to speak to Americans, understand TV programs in English, and find a job that requires English. First, ...

4. Write another paragraph about your plans for developing good study habits. Are you going to come to school every day? Are you going to arrive on time? What are other things you are going to do?

5. Ask members of your team to edit your paragraphs. Then, rewrite them.

6. Read your paragraphs to your team.

7. As a team, design a goal chart that you can each put in your home to remind you of your goals.

8. Present your calendar, paragraphs, and goal chart to the class.

Stand Out 1 Vocabulary List

Pre-Unit
Greetings P2
Numbers P5
Study verbs
listen P7
read P7
speak P7
write P7

Unit 1
Personal information
age 2
divorced 2
height 4
marital status 2
married 2
single 2
weight 4
Hairstyle
bald 6
curly 6
long 6
short 6
straight 6
wavy 6
Family
aunt 8
brother 8
children 8
daughter 8
father 8
granddaughter 8
grandfather 8
grandmother 8
grandson 8
husband 8
mother 8
nephew 8
niece 8
parents 8
sister 8
son 8
uncle 8
wife 8
Hobbies
books 10
computers 10
games 10
movies 10
music 10
parks 10
restaurants 10
sports 10
TV 10

Unit 2
Stores
bookstore 22
clothing store 22
convenience store 22
department store 22
shoe store 22
supermarket 22
Money
bill 25
cash 32
check 26
credit card 32
dime 25
nickel 25
penny 25
quarter 25
Clothing
baseball cap 25
belt 30
blouse 25
coat 25
dress 25
hat 25
pants 30
sandal 30
shirt 30
shorts 30
skirt 25
socks 25
suit 25
sweater 25
tennis shoes 25
tie 25
t-shirt 25
Colors
black 30
blue 30
brown 30
green 30
orange 30
red 30
white 30
yellow 30
Adjectives
big 33
checked 33
large 33
little 33
medium 30
new 33
small 30
striped 33
used 33

Unit 3
Food and meals
apples 45
avocados 44
bread 45
breakfast 41
carrots 44
cereal 42
cheeseburger 53
cookies 45
cucumbers 45
dinner 41
eggs 42
french fries 42
fried chicken 42
ground beef 44
hamburger 42
hot dog 53
lunch 41
milk 44
mustard 45
oranges 45
peanut butter 44
potato chips 45
roast beef 42
salad 53
sandwich 42
side order 53
soda 44
spaghetti 42
toast 42
tomatoes 44
yogurt 45
Containers/Measurements
bag 48
bottle 48
box 48
can 48
gallon 45
jar 48
ounce 54
package 48
pound 45

Unit 4
Housing
apartment 61
backyard 66
balcony 66
bathroom 65
bedroom 65
carport 66
condominium 61
deck 66
dining room 65

driveway 66
electricity 68
family room 66
first floor 66
front porch 66
front yard 66
garage 66
gas 68
hall 66
kitchen 65
living room 65
mobile home 61
second floor 66
single-family home 61
stairs 66
swimming pool 66
utilities 68
yard 66
Furniture
bathtub 73
bed 73
chair 73
coffee table 73
end table 73
lamp 73
painting 73
refrigerator 73
sofa 73
trash can 74

Unit 5
Place in the community
bank 82
bus station 85
city hall 81
dentist's office 82
doctor's office 82
DMV (Department of
   Motor Vehicles) 82
fire station 82
high school 84
hospital 82
hostel 82
hotel 82
library 81
mall 86
motel 82
museum 86
park 81
playground 82
police station 82
post office 82
public schools 82
tennis courts 82
zoo 84

Directions
around the corner 88
between 88
go straight 84
next to 88
on the corner 88
straight ahead 84
turn left 84
turn around 84
turn right 84

Unit 6
Body parts
arm 102
back 102
chest 102
ear 102
eyes 102
foot (feet) 102
hand 102
head 102
leg 102

mouth 102
nose 102
stomach 102
tooth (teeth) 102
Health
ambulance 111
backache 107
cold 107
cough 107
emergency 111
fever 104
flu 104
headache 104
lozenges 107
muscle ache 105
runny nose 104
pain reliever 107
sore throat 104
syrup 107
stomachache 106
temperature 104

Unit 7
Jobs
artist 122
busboy 125
cook/chef 122
homemaker 122
mail carrier 125
mechanic 121
nurse 121
office worker 121
server 121
teller 121
Employment
application 124
benefits 124
cashier 122
custodian 122
experience 124
full-time 124
interview 130
part-time 124

secretary 122
teacher 122

Unit 8
Education
adult program 147
Associate's Degree 147
Bachelor's Degree 147
college 147
degree 147
diploma 147
GED (General Education
    Development) 147
goal 152
junior college 147
life skills 146
trade school 147
university 147

Stand Out 1 Irregular Verb List

The verbs below are used in *Stand Out 1* and have irregular past tense forms.

Base Verb	Simple Past	Base Verb	Simple Past
be	was, were	give	gave
bring	brought	go	went
build	built	have	had
buy	bought	make	made
choose	chose	meet	met
come	came	put	put
do	did	read	read
drive	drove	see	saw
drink	drank	send	sent
draw	drew	sleep	slept
eat	ate	speak	spoke
feel	felt	teach	taught
find	found	write	wrote

Useful Words

Cardinal numbers

1	one
2	two
3	three
4	four
5	five
6	six
7	seven
8	eight
9	nine
10	ten
11	eleven
12	twelve
13	thirteen
14	fourteen
15	fifteen
16	sixteen
17	seventeen
18	eighteen
19	nineteen
20	twenty
21	twenty-one
30	thirty
40	forty
50	fifty
60	sixty
70	seventy
80	eighty
90	ninety
100	one hundred
1000	one thousand
10,000	ten thousand
100,000	one hundred thousand
1,000,00	one million

Ordinal numbers

first	1st	
second	2nd	
third	3rd	
fourth	4th	
fifth	5th	
sixth	6th	
seventh	7th	
eighth	8th	
ninth	9th	
tenth	10th	
eleventh	11th	
twelfth	12th	
thirteenth	13th	
fourteenth	14th	
fifteenth	15th	
sixteenth	16th	
seventeenth	17th	
eighteenth	18th	
nineteenth	19th	
twentieth	20th	
twenty-first	21st	

Days of the week

Sunday
Monday
Tuesday
Wednesday
Thursday
Friday
Saturday

Seasons

winter
spring
summer
fall

Months of the year

January
February
March
April
May
June
July
August
September
October
November
December

Write the date

April 5, 2004 = 4/ 5/ 04

Temperature chart

Degrees Celcius (ºC) and
Degrees Fahrenheit (ºF)

100ºC	212ºF
30ºC	86ºF
25ºC	77ºF
20ºC	68ºF
15ºC	59ºF
10ºC	50ºF
5ºC	41ºF
0ºC	32ºF
–5ºC	23ºF

Weights and measures

Weights:
1 pound (lb.) = 453.6 grams (g)
16 ounces (oz.) = 1 pound (lb.)
1 pound (lb.) = .45 kilogram (kg)

Liquid of Volume
1 cup (c.) = .24 liter (l)
2 cups (c.) = 1 pint (pt.)
2 pints = 1 quart (qt.)
4 quarts = 1 gallon (gal.)
1 gallon (gal.) = 3.78 liters (l)

Length:
1 inch (in. or ″) = 2.54 centimeters (cm)
1 foot (ft. or ′) = .3048 meters (m)
12 inches (12″) = 1 foot (1′)
1 yard (yd.) = 3 feet (3′) or 0.9144 meters (m)
1 mile (mi.) = 1609.34 meters (m) or 1.609 kilometers (km)

Time:
60 seconds = 1 minute
60 minutes = 1 hour
24 hours = 1 day
28-31 days = 1 month
12 months = 1 year

Simple Present: *Be*

Subject	*Be*	Information	Example sentence
I	am	43 years old	I **am** 43 years old.
he, she	is	single	He **is** single. (Roberto **is** single.)
we, you, they	are	from Argentina single married from Russia	She **is** from Argentina. (Gabriela **is** from Argentina.) We **are** single. You **are** married. They **are** from Russia.

Simple Present

Subject	Verb	Example sentence
I, you, we, they	eat like need want make	I **eat** tacos for lunch. You **like** eggs for breakfast. We **need** three cans of corn. They **want** three boxes of cookies. I **make** sandwiches for lunch.
he, she, it	eats likes needs wants makes	He **eats** pizza for dinner. She **likes** tomato soup. He **needs** three pounds of tomatoes. She **wants** two bottles of water. She **makes** sandwiches for Duong.

Simple Present

Subject	Verb	Example sentence
it my leg my arm my foot my head	hurts	My leg **hurts.** My arm **hurts.** My head **hurts.**
they my legs my arms my feet my ears	hurt	My legs **hurt.** My feet **hurt.** My ears **hurt.**

Simple Present

Subject	Verb	Example sentence
I, you, we, they	work	I **work** in an office.
he, she, it	works	He **works** in a restaurant.

Negative Simple Present

Subject	Negative	Verb	Example sentence
I, you, we, they	do not (don't)	work	I **don't work** in an office. You **don't work** in a restaurant.
he, she, it	does not (doesn't)		He **doesn't work** in a school. She **doesn't work** in a hospital.

Simple Present: *Have*

Subject	*Have*	Example sentence
I, you, we, they	have	I **have** a headache. You **have** a sore throat.
he, she, it	has	She **has** a stomachache. He **has** a fever.

Negative Simple Present: *Have*

Subject	Negative	*Have*	Example sentence
I, you, we, they	do not (don't)	have	I **don't have** a headache. You **don't have** a sore throat.
he, she, it	does not (doesn't)	have	She **doesn't have** a stomachache. He **doesn't have** a fever.

Simple Present

Subject	Adverb	Verb	Example sentence
I	always often sometimes rarely never	write	I always **write** postcards.
he, she, it		eats	He rarely **eats** here.
you, we, they		read	They never **read** the newspaper.

Simple Present: *Be*

Subject	*Be*		Example sentence
I	am	early late on time punctual	I **am** always early.
he, she, it	is		He **is** sometimes late. She **is** a good worker.
we, you, they	are		We **are** often early. You **are** never on time. They **are** always punctual.

Be Verb (Questions)

Question words	*Be*	Singular or plural noun	Example question
how much (money)	is	the dress the suit	How much **is** the dress? How much **is** the suit?
how much (money)	are	the socks the ties	How much **are** the socks? How much **are** the ties?

Be Verb (Answers)

Singular or plural noun or pronoun	*Be*	Example answer
it	is	It **is** $48. It**'s** $48. (The dress **is** $48.) It **is** $285. It**'s** $285. (The suit **is** $285.)
they	are	They **are** $12. They**'re** $12. (The socks **are** $12.) They **are** $22. They**'re** $22. (The ties **are** $22.)

Questions and Yes/No Answers

Question	Yes	No
Do you want a hamburger?	Yes, I do.	No, I don't. Thank you.
Do they want sandwiches?	Yes, they do.	No, they don't.
Does he want a sandwich?	Yes, he does.	No, he doesn't.
Does she want a sandwich?	Yes, she does.	No, she doesn't.

Questions with *Can*

Can	Subject	Base verb	Example question
can	I you	help ask talk answer call	**Can** I help you? **Can** I ask you a question? **Can** I talk to you? **Can** you answer a question? **Can** you call me?

Present Continuous

Subject	*Be* Verb	Base + *ing*	Example sentence
I	am	talk + *ing*	I **am talking** on the phone.
you, we, they	are	read+ *ing* call + *ing*	We **are calling** for an appointment.
he, she, it	is	move + *ing*	She **is moving** into a new apartment.

Present Continuous

Subject	*Be*	Base + *ing*	Time	Example sentence
I	am (I'm)	writing	right now today	I**'m writing** a letter right now.
he, she, it	is (she's)	eating		She**'s eating** a sandwich.
you, we, they	are (they're)	reading		They**'re reading** a book today.

Should

Subject	*Should*	Base verb	Example sentence
I, you, he, she, it, we, they	should	rest	You **should** rest.
		stay	He **should** stay home.
		go	They **should** see a doctor.
		take	I **should** take pain relievers.
			We **should** take cough syrup.

Should (Negative)

Subject	Should	Base verb	Example sentence
I, you, he, she, it, we, they	should not (shouldn't)	drive	You **shouldn't** drive and take this medicine.
		drink	He **shouldn't** drink alcohol with this medicine.
		go	We **shouldn't** go out.

Simple Past: Regular Verbs

Subject	Base verb + *ed*		Example sentence
I, you, he, she, it, we, they	cleaned	tables	I **cleaned** tables.
	cooked	hamburgers	You **cooked** hamburgers.
	prepared	breakfast	He **prepared** breakfast.
	delivered	packages	She **delivered** packages.
	counted	the money	It **counted** the money.
	helped	other workers	We **helped** other workers.
	moved	to the United States	They **moved** to the United States.

Simple Past: *Be*

Subject	Be		Example sentence
I, he, she, it	was	a mail carrier	I **was** a mail carrier.
we, you, they	were	happy	You **were** happy.

Simple Past: *Be*

Subject	Be		Example sentence
I, he, she, it	was	early, late	I **was** early yesterday. He **was** often late. She **was** always a good worker.
we, you, they	were	on time, punctual	We **were** early on Saturday. You **were** on time today. They **were** never punctual.

Regular Past Tense Verbs

Base	Simple past
study	studied
participate	participated
help	helped
listen	listened
watch	watched
practice	practiced
learn	learned

Irregular Past Tense Verbs

Base	Simple past
come	came
see	saw
write	wrote
speak	spoke
read	read
teach	taught

Verb + Infinitive

Subject	Verb	Infinitive	Example sentence
I, you, we, they	like want need	to read to travel to work to talk to handle to study	I like **to read.** You want **to travel.** We need **to work** alone. They like **to talk** on the phone.
he, she, it	likes wants needs		He likes **to handle** money. She wants **to study.**

Verb + Noun

Subject	Verb	Noun	Example sentence
I, you, we, they	like want need	cars computer books school food	I like **cars.** You want a **computer.** We need **books.** They like **school.**
he, she, it	likes wants needs		He likes **computers.** She wants **food.**

Future with *Going to*

Subject	*Going to*	Base verb	Example sentence
I	am going to (I'm going to)	learn listen practice read speak study write	I **am going to** learn English.
you, we, they	are going to (you're/we're/ they're going to)		We **are going to** practice English.
he, she, it	is going to (he's/she's going to)		She **is going to** speak English.

Future with *Will*

Subject	*Will*	Base	Example sentence
I, you,	will	study	I **will** study every day.
he, she, it		work	She **will** work hard.
we, they		get married	They **will** get married.

Stand Out 1 Listening Scripts

PRE-UNIT
CD 1, Track 1, Page P1
A. Listen.

| Hi! | How are you? |
| Hello! | Fine! How are you? |

Welcome to our class.

CD 1, Track 2, Page P2
D. Listen and complete the conversation.
Roberto: Hi. I'm Roberto. How are you?
Gabriela: Hello. My name is Gabriela. I'm fine, thanks.
Roberto: Welcome to our class.
Gabriela: Thank you.
Roberto: Our teacher is Miss Smith.

CD 1, Track 3, Page P3
E. Listen and repeat.
Hi! I'm Gabriela. G-A-B-R-I-E-L-A.
Hello. I'm Duong. D-U-O-N-G.

CD 1, Track 4, Page P3
F. Listen and repeat.
A B C D E F G H I J K L M
N O P Q R S T U V W X Y Z

CD 1, Track 5, Page P3
G. Listen and write.
1. Hi! I'm Susan.
2. Hello! My name is Bill.
3. How are you? I'm Ana.
4. Hi! My name is Tony.

CD 1, Track 6, Page P5
C. Listen and practice saying the numbers 0 to 20.

CD 1, Track 7, Page P5
D. Listen and write the numbers you hear.
1. five
2. eight
3. **Duong:** Hello, Gabriela.
Gabriela: Hi, Duong.
Duong: How many students are in your class?
Gabriela: I think there are nine.
4. **Duong:** My class is bigger.
Gabriela: Really? How many?
Duong: We have 19 students.
5. **Duong:** Maybe my class is bigger because it is shorter.
Gabriela: How long is your class?
Duong: It is two hours a day.
6. **Gabriela:** Is that all?
Duong: Yes, that's all.
Gabriela: My class is three hours a day.

CD 1, Track 8, Page P5
E. Listen and write the missing numbers.
My name is Gabriela. My address is 14 Main Street. The zip code is 06119. My phone number is 401-555-7248. There are nine students in my class.

CD 1, Track 9, Page P7
B. Listen and point to the correct picture.
1. I am a busy man. I have to write everything down that

I do and that I need to do. I write everything to stay organized.
2. I am a happy person. I speak to my friends every day. I also think it is important to speak English in the United States.
3. I like to listen to music. When I listen to music in English, I learn a lot.
4. I read every chance I get. I read on the bus, at lunch, and in the classroom.

CD 1, Track 10, Page P8
E. Listen and follow the instructions.
Please stand. Please sit down. Please read page one in your book. Please listen carefully. Please take out a sheet of paper. Please write your name on a sheet of paper.
CD 1, Track 11
John and Maria are good students. They write information in their books. They read English regularly. They stand up in class and speak when they have the opportunity. They follow instructions and sit, stand, write, speak, and everything else the teacher asks.

UNIT 1
CD 1, Track 12, Page 2
D. Listen and complete the missing information.
1. Eva Malinska is happy to be in the United States. She wants to learn English. In Warsaw, Poland, she learned a bit of English. She wants to help other people in her family learn English. She is divorced and 60 years old.
CD 1, Track 13
2. Gabriela Ramirez is 26. She listens to the radio and reads the newspaper every day. She wants to learn English quickly. She is single and from Buenos Aires, Argentina.
CD 1, Track 14
3. Felipe Rodriguez is a student and also works hard. He is a salesperson and goes to school at night. He is 33 years old. He is married with three kids. He talks to his family in Cuba once a week.

CD 1, Track 15, Page 5
D. Listen and complete the chart.
1. **A:** Excuse me. I am looking for Roberto Garcia.
B: I don't think I know him. What does he look like?
A: He has black hair and brown eyes, I think.
B: And his height . . . how tall is he?
A: He is five feet, eleven inches tall. He is probably 43 years old.
B: Oh, he's in Room 114.
A: Thanks!
CD 1, Track 16
2. **A:** Do you see Trinh over there?
B: I don't see her.
A: She is 5 feet, 1 inch tall and has black hair and brown eyes.
B: Oh, I see her now. Is she about 33 years old?
A: That sounds right.
CD 1, Track 17
3. **A:** Excuse me. I am looking for Gabriela Ramirez. She is tall, maybe 5 feet 5 inches. She has black hair and brown eyes. She is 26 years old.
B: No, I haven't seen her.

4. A: My name is Alan.
B: Please describe yourself.
A: I am 5 feet 9 inches tall. I have red hair and green eyes. I am 64 years old.

CD 1, Track 19, Page 5
E. Listen to the conversation.
A: What does Roberto look like?
B: He has black hair and brown eyes.
A: How tall is he?
B: He is five feet, eleven inches tall.
A: Thank you.

CD 1, Track 20, Page 7
A. Listen to the conversation.
Roberto: Duong, this is my mother, my father, and my sister.
Antonio: Nice to meet you, Duong. Where are you from?
Duong: I'm from Vietnam.
Antonio: Do your parents live here in the United States?
Duong: No, right now they live in Vietnam.

CD 1, Track 21, Page 8
D. Look at the picture and write the names on the family tree. Then, listen to check your answers.
   My name is Roberto Garcia. I am very happily married. My wife's name is Silvia. This is a picture of my family. The older man and the woman in the picture are my parents. My mother's name is Rebecca and my father's name is Antonio. I have one sister, Lidia, and one brother, Julio. The girl and the boy are my children, Juan and Carla.

CD 1, Track 22, Page 10
A. Listen. Put an *R* by things Roberto likes and an *S* by things Silvia likes.
   Roberto and Silvia are happily married. Roberto likes movies, games, and books. Silvia likes parks, restaurants, and music. They both like sports, computers, and TV.

CD 1, Track 23, Page 14
F. Listen and write Juan's schedule.
   Juan is a good student. He wants to learn English so he can get a better job. He has a regular schedule and follows it every day. He eats breakfast every morning from 6:00 to 6:30. He usually eats cereal, but sometimes he has eggs. Directly after he eats, he reads the newspaper. He usually reads in English from 6:30 to 6:45. He listens to the radio on the way to school from 7:00 A.M. to 7:25 A.M. He writes in his journal before class from 7:30 to 8:00. He practices English in class from 8:00 to 10:00 A.M. Monday through Friday.

UNIT 2
CD 1, Track 24, Page 22
D. Listen to Van and her husband. Circle the best place to get each item.
Van: I need some things for school. Do you want to shop for me?
Nam: No, not today. I have things here to do at home.
Van: OK, where can I go for these things?
Nam: What do you need?
Van: I need sneakers, shirts, bread, cheese, and fruit for lunches, a radio, and a bilingual dictionary.
Nam: Wow! That sounds like a lot.
Van: I know.

Nam: The best place for shoes is Martin's Department Store. You can buy shirts at Martin's also. You can also buy a good radio at Martin's.
Nam: All at Martin's?
Van: Yes, it's a good place for many things, but you need to go to Hero Books for the dictionary, and Sam's Food Mart around the corner has all you need for lunches.

CD 1, Track 25, Page 24
C. Listen and circle the amounts you hear.
EXAMPLE: How much is it? It's $22.50.
1. That's $34.15.
2. Here's $33.00.
3. That comes to $15.70.
4. The total cost is $77.95.

CD 1, Track 26, Page 24
D. Listen and write the prices.
1. Customer: Excuse me. How much is the vacuum?
Salesperson: It's $98.99 on sale.
Customer: Thanks, I'll take it.
2. Customer: Excuse me. Can you help me? I'm looking for a washing machine.
Salesperson: This is a good brand.
Customer: Is that right? OK, how much is it?
Salesperson: It's four hundred and fifty dollars.
Customer: Four hundred and fifty dollars? That much?
Salesperson: I'm afraid so.
3. Customer: I just want this candy bar.
Salesperson: That will be $1.25, please.
Customer: Here you go—one dollar and twenty-five cents.
4. Customer: I want to buy a ream of white paper.
Salesperson: The paper is over there. It's $6.50.
Customer: Thank you.
5. Customer: Every time I buy a telephone, I get a bad one. Maybe I should buy an expensive one.
Salesperson: How about this one for $80?

CD 1, Track 27, Page 27
A. Write the correct letter under each type of clothing. Then, listen for the missing prices.
   We have many good deals at Dress for Less. Be sure to come in. Socks are $12, ties are $22, and suits are $285. Our dresses are $48, and our skirts are $35! We have great deals on sweaters at $36, and women's hats are $38. Don't miss our great deals!

CD 1, Track 28, Page 30
A. Listen and point to the clothing you hear about in the conversation.
Roberto: Gabriela, what are you wearing to class today?
Gabriela: I think I will wear my white blouse. How about you?
Roberto: I'll wear my red t-shirt. And I think I will go casual and wear shorts.
Gabriela: Me, too, I want to go casual. I am wearing my blue pants with a black belt.
Roberto: You won't miss me. I will be wearing a baseball cap.

CD 1, Track 29, Page 34
C. Listen to the conversation with your books closed. What does Tatsuya want to buy?
Tatsuya: Excuse me. I want a TV.
Salesperson: A big TV or a small TV?
Tatsuya: I want a small TV.

Salesperson: OK, how about this one?
Tatsuya: Yes, that's good. How much is it?
Salesperson: It's $135.00.
Tatsuya: I'll take it!

CD 1, Track 30, Page 35
G. Listen to the conversations and circle the correct answers.
1. Tatsuya: Excuse me. I want a TV.
Salesperson: A big TV or a small TV?
Tatsuya: I want a small TV.
Salesperson: OK, how about this one?
Tatsuya: Yes, that's good. How much is it?
Salesperson: It's $135.00.
Tatsuya: I'll take it!
CD 1, Track 31
2. Emily: We need to move.
Steve: I know. What do you want? Do you want a new house or an old house?
Emily: Well, I am not sure. They both have benefits. I guess I want an old house.
Steve: OK, we want an old house, right?
CD 1, Track 32
3. Nancy: I am here to buy a blouse for my friend Gabriela.
Salesperson: OK, do you know her size?
Nancy: She wants a medium blouse, I think.
Sales person: Step over here, and we will see what we can find in a medium blouse.
CD 1, Track 33
4. Ivan: I want a new car.
Natasha: I want a new car, too.
Ivan: They are expensive.
Natasha: How can we afford it?
Ivan: I guess we want a new car, but we will have to wait to buy one.

CD 1, Track 34, Page 36
A. Listen and write the prices in Column 1.
The TV is $456.78.   The shoes are $28.98.
The CD player is $98.45.   The dictionary is $18.95.
The shirt is $24.50.   The sweater is $33.99.
The vacuum is $168.   The shorts are $17.00.

UNIT 3
CD 1, Track 35, Page 42
E. Listen to Dave and check the information in Exercise D.
   Hello, my name is Dave. I am a teacher at Alexander Adult School. I eat lunch here. They have a cafeteria. I teach all day so I can eat here for all three meals. For breakfast before class, I eat eggs, cereal, and toast. For lunch after my first class, I eat a hamburger and french fries. Sometimes, I eat a sandwich for lunch instead of a hamburger. For dinner, I either have spaghetti, roast beef, or fried chicken. Spaghetti is my favorite.

CD 1, Track 36, Page 44
B. Listen to Duong and his wife, Minh, make a shopping list. What do they need to buy? Write *yes* or *no*.
Duong: We need to go shopping. We are out of everything.
Minh: You're right. Let's make a shopping list.
Duong: Well, I know we need ground beef.
Minh: That's not all. We really need carrots and tomatoes, too.
Duong: OK, I'll write that down—carrots and tomatoes.
Minh: Let's buy some soda, too.

Duong: OK, I'll add it to the list.
Minh: Wow! Avocados are expensive. Let's just buy two.
Duong: OK, two it is. Anything else?
Minh: No, I think that is it.
Duong: OK. I have ground beef, carrots, tomatoes, soda, and avocados on the list.

CD 1, Track 37, Page 47
C. Listen to the conversation between Duong and Minh. What do they need at the supermarket? Check the foods.
Duong: It is too expensive to buy food at school every day. I have the same sandwiches every week. Maybe we should buy something different, but I need something healthy.
Minh: OK. What did you have in mind?
Duong: Well, I thought I might try tuna fish. It is delicious.
Minh: Yes, they say fish is good for you, too. What about chicken?
Duong: Chicken is OK, but I don't have time to prepare it.
Minh: We can buy it in slices. You don't need to prepare it.
Duong: Great. I also need peanut butter and jelly.
Minh: Yes, we do need both. We are completely out.

CD 1, Track 38, Page 52
I. Listen to Sebastien ask about prices. Complete the charts.
Sebastien: Excuse me. I see that you have a special deal where if a customer finds a cheaper price at a different store, you will give him the same deal. Is that right?
Salesperson: That's right. Do you have a newspaper ad?
Sebastien: Yes. It says right here that at Puente Market, bananas are ninety-two cents a pound. Here at Food City, they are ninety-eight cents.
Salesperson: That looks right. We will give you the deal.
Sebastien: Here are more examples. Puente Market is always cheaper.
Salesperson: Let's see. You're right. Oranges at Puente Market are $2.20 a pound and at Food City, they cost $2.39 a pound. Pears at Puente Market are $1.29 a pound. Here at Food City, they are $1.39.
Sebastien: Look at this! Apples are $2.00 at Food City and only $1.49 at Puent Market.
Salesperson: Wow. It looks like we need to change a lot of prices!

CD 1, Tracks 39, Page 54
E. Listen to the orders. Write each student's order in the chart below. Write the prices from the picture above.
1. Manny's order
Manny: I want a cheeseburger, a green salad, and an orange juice please.
Server: No orange juice today. Would you like milk or soda?
Manny: A soda please.
Server: OK, two minutes. Next.
CD 1, Track 40
2. Tran's order
Tran: What sandwiches do you have?
Server: Ham or cheese.
Tran: I'll have a ham sandwich.
Server: OK.
Tran: And a green salad, too.
Server: Of course. What about a drink?
Tran: No, thanks.
Server: OK. That's a ham sandwich and a green salad, right?
Tran: That's right. Thanks.
CD 1, Track 41
3. Miyuki's order

Miyuki: I want some milk, please, and a hot dog.
Server: Do you want mustard?
Miyuki: No, thanks. Just french fries.
Server: That's fine. Hot dog, no mustard, french fries, and a milk coming up.

UNIT 4
CD 1, Track 42, Page 61
A. Study the pie chart about housing in Corbin. Listen and write the numbers.

Corbin is a thriving community. It is growing very quickly because of its perfect location between the ocean and the mountains, and its terrific climate.

Corbin is mostly a residential community. There are approximately 15,000 houses in the city. There are less than half as many apartments. There are around 7,000 apartments. There are also a handful of mobile home parks with a total of 350 mobile homes. Finally, there are 1,700 condominiums in the north end of the city.

CD 1, Track 43, Page 64
B. Listen to Saud and the real estate agent. How many bedrooms and bathrooms does Saud need? Then, listen to the other conversations and fill in the information.
1. **Saud:** I'm looking for a house to rent for my family.
Agent: Would you please sit down?
Saud: Thank you.
Agent: How many bedrooms do you need?
Saud: I need three bedrooms and one bathroom.
Agent: I think we can help you.
CD 1, Track 44
2. **Silvia:** We're interested in a nice apartment in the city.
Agent: I'm sure we can help you. This one has two bedrooms and two bathrooms. Is that OK?
Silvia: Maybe. What's the rent?
Agent: It's only $850 a month.
Silvia: $850 a month? This is going to be more difficult than I thought.
CD1, Track 45
3. **Tien:** Do you have any properties for a big family?
Agent: Well, let's see.
Tien: I think I need a house with four bedrooms.
Agent: To buy or rent?
Tien: To rent, I think. How much are the rentals here?
Agent: We have one here with two bathrooms for $1,300 a month.
Tien: Can we go out and look at it?
Agent: Yes, of course.
CD 1, Track 46
4. **Felipe:** What do you have in terms of one-bedroom apartments?
Agent: We have a one-bedroom apartment on Sycamore Street.
Felipe: That looks great. How much is the rent?
Agent: It's $750 a month, plus utilities.
Felipe: Is it one bathroom, too?
Agent: That's right, one bathroom and one bedroom.

CD 1, Track 47, Page 68
F. Listen and write the letter of the classified ad above.
1. This apartment is a large three-bedroom apartment with lots of good features. There is a pool. All utilities are paid, and it's near a school. Come and see. You won't be sorry.
2. Apartments come and go, but this is the best. It has three bedrooms, and it's only $800 a month. It's on the second floor so you can enjoy a beautiful balcony.

3. This great apartment is far from city traffic. Hot summers are no problem. We have air-conditioning, and we pay the electricity. Call Margaret at 555-2672.
4. This is a bargain! Seven hundred dollars a month to lease this one-bedroom, one-bath apartment. No pets please! Call our manager, Fred. He will get you in today! 555-7164.

CD 1, Track 48, Page 70
B. Match the questions with the answers. Then, listen and check your answers.
Agent: Hello, Your Home Realty. This is Ana.
Saud: Hello, I am looking for an apartment to rent. Do you have any three bedrooms?
Agent: Yes. I have one that is beautiful and like new.
Saud: Really? How is the neighborhood?
Agent: It is quiet, and there is a school nearby.
Saud: That sounds good. I have a dog. Are pets OK?
Agent: Yes, as a matter of fact, they are.
Saud: Is it on the first floor?
Agent: No, it's on the third floor.
Saud: That will be a bit difficult. Does it have air-conditioning?
Agent: Yes, it does.
Saud: Is it expensive? How much is the rent?
Agent: It's $1,200 a month.
Saud: When can I see the apartment?
Agent: Today at 3:00 would be great if you are free.
Saud: Sounds good to me. See you then.
Agent: OK, bye.

CD 1, Track 49, Page 71
D. Listen to the conversations. Complete the chart.
1. **Owner:** Hello. Can I help you?
Saud: Yes, I am calling about the condominium for rent.
Owner: How can I help you?
Saud: How much is the rent?
Owner: It's $1,200 a month.
Saud: When can I see it?
Owner: How about today at 3:00?
Saud: Great! Thank you.
CD 1, Track 50
2. **Owner:** Hello. Can I help you?
Saud: Yes, I am calling about the apartment for rent that I saw in the paper. Is it still available?
Owner: Yes, we are renting it for $1,450.
Saud: Wow! That sounds expensive.
Owner: Maybe, but it is a beautiful and new apartment.
Saud: OK, when can I see it?
Owner: You can stop by at 10 A.M.
CD 1, Track 51
3. **Owner:** Hello.
Saud: Hi. I am calling about the house for rent. Are you the owner?
Owner: Yes, I am. What would you like to know?
Saud: How much is the rent?
Owner: It's $2,000. It's a four bedroom.
Saud: I don't know if I need something that big. When can I see it?
Owner: Come by at 3:30.
Saud: OK, see you then.
CD 1, Track 52
4. **Saud:** Hello.
Owner: Hello. Is this Saud?
Saud: Yes, that's me.
Owner: I am returning your call about the two-bedroom

apartment.
Saud: Oh, yes. How much is the rent?
Owner: It's $900 a month.
Saud: Great. Can I come by today.
Owner: Of course. Come by around 2:00.
Saud: Thanks, I will.

CD 1, Track 53, Page 75
G. Look at the living room. Follow the instructions.
1. Draw a window and a door.
2. Put a painting on the wall.
3. Put a sofa under the painting.
4. Put a chair between the sofa and the door.
5. Put a coffee table in the middle of the room.
6. Draw an end table next to the chair in the corner.
7. Draw a lamp on the end table.

UNIT 5
CD 2, Track 1, Page 82
D. Listen. Write the number under the correct picture.
1. This is a place where people mail letters and packages, and they buy stamps.
2. This is a place with trained workers who help the community when there is an emergency, such as a fire.
3. This is a place where very sick people go for surgery and other problems. Sometimes people go here in an emergency. They sometimes come by ambulance.
4. This is a place where people go to get a driver's license and identification.
5. This is a place where people put their money. Sometimes they get a checking account and sometimes they get credit cards and loans.
6. This is a place where police officers work. It is the police officers' office.

CD 2, Track 2, Page 83
E. Listen to the conversation. Practice the conversation with new information.
Emanuela: I need to call the hospital.
Lisa: Why?
Emanuela: My sister is very sick.
Lisa: The number is 555-7665.

CD 2, Track 3, Page 86
H. Listen and check the boxes for the words you hear.
1. A: Can you give me directions, please?
B: Maybe. Where do you want to go?
A: I am looking for the mall.
B: It's on Broadway. Turn around and go straight for two blocks. Turn right on Hamilton Avenue. You will see it.
A: Thanks!
CD 2, Track 4
2. A: Excuse me. Do you know the way to the post office?
B: Yes, of course. Go straight ahead two miles. Turn left on Maple.
CD 2, Track 5
3. A: I am totally confused. Where is the movie theater from here?
B: It is very close.
A: Can you give me directions?
B: Sure. Turn left on First Street. Then, go straight ahead three blocks.
A: Thanks so much.
CD 2, Track 6
4. A: Can I help you find something?
B: Yes, I am looking for the museum. I hear there is a great

dinosaur exhibit there.
A: Yes, that's right. It is on Main Street.
B: Where is Main Street?
A: Turn right and go three blocks.
B: Thank you.
CD 2, Track 7
5. A: Where is the park?
B: Turn around and go straight for six blocks. You can't miss it.
A: Are you sure?
B: I am absolutely positive.

CD 2, Track 8, Page 88
C. Study the directory with your classmates and teacher. Listen for prepositions.
A: Well, it's time to go to the mall.
B: I love shopping.
A: What do you need?
B: I want a new dress.
A: Oh, you should go to Casual Woman. It's next to Sport Runner.
B: Sounds good. Do you want to eat?
A: Yes, I do. Where would you suggest we go?
B: I don't know. Maybe Jay's Hamburger around the corner.
A: Great! I will meet you there. First, I need to go to Landsbury Music and buy a CD.
B: Where is that?
A: It's on the corner outside.
B: Oh, that's right. I remember.
A: OK, I'll see you at Jay's. Where is it again?
B: It's between The Real Thing and Ryan's Suit and Tie.
A: OK. See you later.

CD 2, Track 9, Page 90
C. Listen to Gabriela leave a message. Circle the answers.
Machine: Hello, this is David. I can't come to the phone right now, but your call is very important. Please leave a message after the tone and I will get back to you right away.
Gabriela: This is Gabriela. I want to go to the post office tomorrow. Can you go with me? I hope so. I need some help from a friend. Call me back at 555-3765.

CD 2, Track 10, Page 95
F. Listen. Then, answer the questions.
1. Where do you go to school?
2. Where do you live?
3. Where is a restaurant nearby?
4. What do you sometimes do?

CD 2, Track 11, Page 97
C. Listen to the messages. Complete the chart.
1. Machine: This is Herman. I can't come to the phone right now. Please leave a message.
Nadia: This is Nadia. I have a question. My number is 555-2344.
2. Machine: This is Herman. I can't come to the phone right now. Please leave a message.
Vien: This is Vien. I want to talk. Can you call me? My number is 555-7798.
3. Machine: This is Herman. I can't come to the phone right now. Please leave a message.
David: David here. I need information. Please call 555-1234.
4. Machine: This is Herman. I can't come to the phone right now. Please leave a message.
Ricardo: My name is Ricardo. I need a phone number. My number is 555-7343.

UNIT 6
CD 2, Track 12, Page 102
D. Listen to the patients talk to the doctor. What are their problems? Complete the sentences.
1. Karen: Doctor, thank you for seeing me on such short notice.
Doctor: What seems to be the trouble?
Karen: Well, I'm having trouble with my hand.
Doctor: What do you mean, trouble?
Karen: My hand is very stiff in the morning. I work at a computer, and it is getting very difficult to do my work.
CD 2, Track 13
2. Doctor: How are you today, Roberto?
Roberto: I'm fine except my leg hurts all the time.
Doctor: I see. Let's check it out. Where does it hurt?
Roberto: My leg hurts right here near the knee.
Doctor: We probably should take some X-rays.
CD 2, Track 14
3. Doctor: Well, Tino, it seems like you are here every week these days.
Tino: I guess so doctor. My foot is killing me.
Doctor: I know that you were here last week because of your elbow. Did the prescription help?
Tino: Not at all. It seems to be getting worse.

CD 2, Track 15, Page 104
B. Listen and practice the conversation.
Doctor: What's the matter?
Miguel: Doctor, I feel very sick. I have a terrible sore throat.
Doctor: You have the flu.
Miguel: The flu?
Doctor: Yes, the flu!

CD 2, Track 16, Page 104
C. Listen to each conversation. Circle the problem.
1. Doctor: What's the matter?
Miguel: Doctor, I feel very sick. I have a terrible sore throat.
Doctor: You have the flu.
Miguel: The flu?
Doctor: Yes, the flu!
CD 2, Track 17
2. Doctor: What's the matter?
Patient: I don't know. I am terribly tired.
Doctor: Do you have any other symptoms?
Patient: Yes, I have a fever.
Doctor: Well, let's examine you. Open up and say, "Aahh."
CD 2, Track 18
3. Doctor: What's the matter?
Patient: I have a headache.
Doctor: How long have you had it?
Patient: I have had this headache for one week.
Doctor: This could be serious. Please sit down.
CD 2, Track 19
4. Doctor: What's the matter?
Patient: I have a cold.
Doctor: Maybe I can give you some medicine for that runny nose.
Patient: Yes, I have a terrible runny nose.

CD 2, Track 20, Page 108
G. Listen to Karen reading the medicine labels. Write the medicine for each description.
Well, let me see. The doctor says that I need to take this medicine for the next few days. Here it says, "Take one

lozenge as needed for sore throat pain." I probably will need that. My throat really hurts. I will especially need it at work when I am talking to everyone.
This one says to take two tablespoons every four hours. Let me see, that means I should take one when I wake up around 8:00 and then at noon and again at 4:00. I will take the last tablespoon at 8:00.
This last one reads, "Take two tablets every three hours." I will do that until my headache goes away. I hope that is soon. I really don't like to be sick.

CD 2, Track 21, Page 110
A. Listen and practice the conversation.
Operator: What is the emergency?
Victor: There is a car accident.
Operator: Where is the accident?
Victor: It's on Fourth and Bush.
Operator: What is your name?
Victor: It's Victor Karaskov.
Operator: Is anyone hurt?
Victor: Yes. Please send an ambulance.

CD 2, Track 22, Page 112
F. Listen to the conversations. Complete the sentences.
1. Visitor: Excuse me. Where are the elevators? I can't seem to find them.
Staff: They are down the hall.
Visitor: Where?
Staff: They are close to the restrooms.
Visitor: Thanks.
CD 2, Track 23
2. Staff: Can I help you?
Visitor: Yes. I am looking for the wheelchair entrance. Is it close by?
Staff: Yes, it is. It is through the lobby and to your left.
Visitor: Where? I don't understand.
Staff: It is in the emergency room.
Visitor: Oh, thanks.
CD 2, Track 24
3. Visitor: I need to make a call. Where are the phones?
Staff: The pay phones are close to the entrance.
Visitor: Oh, I see them now. Thanks.
CD 2, Track 25
4. Visitor: Can you help me.
Staff: What can I do for you?
Visitor: I am looking for Information.
Staff: This is Information.
Visitor: Right here in the lobby?
Staff: Yes. Information is in the lobby.

CD 2, Track 26, Page 114
E. Listen to the conversations about exercise. Write the number under the correct picture.
1. A: I am so tired.
B: Why?
A: I think I need to exercise more. I don't feel very healthy.
B: I swim every day at the gym. It is great exercise.
A: Maybe I'll try that.
CD 2, Track 27
2. Husband: I don't get any exercise.
Wife: Yes you do.
Husband: What do you mean? I never even leave the house.
Wife: You vacuum every day. That is exercise.
Husband: Oh, I never thought of that.

CD 2, Track 28
3. A: What do you do for exercise?
B: I jog.
A: What is jogging?
B: I run slowly and enjoy nature with my dog.
A: That sounds great.

CD 2, Track 29
4. A: I exercise every day.
B: Me, too.
A: What do you do?
B: I get most of my exercise outside in the yard. Gardening can be good exercise, too.
A: Really.
B: Sure, why not?

UNIT 7
CD 2, Track 30, Page 122
E. Listen to each conversation. Circle the correct job title.
1. Supervisor: Hello, Maria. I have some important work for you today.
Maria: Great. I am ready to work.
Supervisor: One of your secretary responsibilities is to file, so please file all the papers.
Maria: Yes, sir. I will have it finished by lunch.

CD 2, Track 31
2. A: What do you do?
B: I am a cook at Market Street Grill.
A: Wow, that's great. I hear the food is very good there.

CD 2, Track 32
3. A: My job is so great! I love working with people.
B: Me, too. What do you do?
A: I have the perfect job.
B: Well, what is it?
A: I am a teacher at an adult school in Fairmont.

CD 2, Track 33
4. Woman: I'm looking for a job.
Manager: Do you have experience.
Manager: Yes, I do. I worked at the theater down the street for three years.
Manager: What was your job?
Woman: I was a cashier.
Manager: So, you are good with money and making change.
Woman: Yes, I think I do a good job.
Manager: OK, let's get you an application.

CD 2, Track 34, Page 124
C. Listen to the conversations. Bubble in the correct benefits.
1. Supervisor: Roberto, you need to take a vacation right away.
Roberto: Well, I'm not sure I have time.
Manager: If you don't take vacation now, then you will lose it. You have five days.
Roberto: OK, I'll talk to my wife and see what she says.

CD 2, Track 35
2. Anya: I have a problem.
Manager: What can I do for you?
Anya: My husband had an accident.
Manager: An accident? What happened?
Anya: He was in a car accident and broke his leg.
Manager: What can I do?
Anya: Is he covered by my insurance?
Manager: Of course. Your whole family is covered by your insurance.

CD 2, Track 36
3. Steve: I'm sorry. I have to call in sick.

Manager: I'm sorry to hear that.
Steve: Yes, I have a fever. Maybe I have the flu.
Manager: How long will you be out?
Steve: Do you know how much sick leave I have left?
Manager: I'll check on it for you.

CD 2, Track 37, Page 125
E. Listen and write the missing words.
We need a cook for our restaurant in San Francisco. The salary is $12 an hour. You need two years experience for this job. This is a full-time position with benefits. We offer sick leave and a two-week vacation every year. Apply in person at 3500 West Arbor Place, San Francisco, California.

CD 2, Track 38, Page 129
G. Listen and complete the job history. Then, practice the conversation in Exercise F again with the new information.
My name is Nadia. My first job I ever had was as a receptionist. I worked very hard. I did that job for over three years and learned a lot. I talked to people every day on the phone. I started my second position in 2001. I was an office worker. I typed letters all day, every day. Now I am a nurse. I help doctors and people. It is a great job.

CD 2, Track 39, Page 131
C. Listen and complete the conversations with the words from the box.
1. Juan: Excuse me. May I speak to you?
Manager: Please make an appointment.
Juan: Who do I talk to for an appointment?

CD 2, Track 40
2. Juan: Excuse me. May I speak to you?
Manager: Sure. Come in and sit down.
Juan: Thank you.

CD 2, Track 41
3. Juan: Excuse me. May I speak to you?
Manager: Not right now. I'm busy.
Juan: I'm sorry. I can make an appointment.

CD 2, Track 42, Page 135
F. Listen to John's evaluation. Circle the correct rating (needs improvement, good, or superior).
Supervisor: John, I think in time you will become a good worker. You certainly speak well and you are great with the customers. I gave you a *superior* for communication skills. This is why I am sure you can be a great employee in time. I did notice that overall you come on time. You were late once, but only by a few minutes. For punctuality I have given you a *good*.
I know that you are trying to work hard and make extra money through commissions. You will do better if you dress better and keep your hair neat. Do this and you will see your sales soar. For now, I had to give you a *needs improvement* on appearance. You are new so don't worry too much about this last one. You will learn quickly if you apply yourself. I gave you a *needs improvement* for product knowledge. I am sure that will change in no time.

UNIT 8
CD 2, Track 43, Page 142
E. Listen to Angela talk about her study skills. Check the things she did to study.
My name is Angela Sheldon. I am in college now. I studied English in school, so I could go to college here in the United States. I took advantage of every opportunity, so I could learn

quickly. For example, I came to class on time every day. I wrote down new words in my notebook.
I learned new words every day. At home, I watched TV. It was really good for me. I watched the news and other programs. I think the best thing I did was I helped and taught other students. Now I am in college. I am happy to be here.

CD 2, Track 44, Page 146
I. Listen and write the life skills you hear in the conversation. Write them here and in your notebook.
Nadia: English is very important to me. I need to learn it well so I can go to college.
Phuong: You need to study a lot.
Nadia: I know, but school will be out for two months. What can I do?
Phuong: Life is practice.
Nadia: What do you mean?
Phuong: When you read a bus schedule, that is a life skill and you practice English.
Nadia: I see, so reading the newspaper is a life skill, too, right?
Phuong: That's right.
Nadia: How about calling the doctor for an appointment? Is that a life skill?
Phuong: Yes, it is. So is making a notebook.
Nadia: I guess you're right. I can practice English every day. Making this notebook will really help.

CD 2, Track 45, Page 148
D. Listen to the conversations and check the correct information in Exercise C.
1. Ahmed: I want to be a computer technician, but first I need to learn more English.
Counselor: That's very important. Do you have a high school diploma?
Ahmed: No, I don't.
Counselor: Well, that is always a good place to start. Maybe you can get work without it, but it's very important.
Ahmed: Yes, I know. That's one of my plans.
Counselor: You can learn to be a computer technician in a trade school, or you can go to a two-year college.
Ahmed: Which one is better?
Counselor: They are both good, but a trade school will help you find a job later.
CD 2, Track 46
2. Akiko: I want to understand computers in the United States so I can get a good job in Web design.
Counselor: First, you have to speak English very well.
Akiko: If I study at home and come to adult school, I think that will be enough.
Counselor: You should plan to go to college and take technology courses, too. It's hard, but you need the experience.
CD 2, Track 47
3. Counselor: That's great that you want to be a teacher.
Minh: Yes, but I do need to learn English.
Counselor: That's right. You have your high school diploma, so you can start at a two-year college or go right to the university.
Minh: Which is better for me?
Counselor: They are both good. The college is cheaper and you can take English classes while you take other classes.
CD 2, Track 48
4. Counselor: Alan, you want to be a cook, right?
Alan: That's right.
Counselor: Do you want to be a chef in an expensive restaurant where you can make special food?
Alan: I don't know. I like to cook. Is it hard to be a chef?

Counselor: You need to go to school—maybe a trade school.
Alan: That sounds like a lot of work, but I'll think about it.
CD 2, Track 49
5. Mario: I just need a little English and I can go to work. I am already a good mechanic.
Counselor: Do you have a GED or high school diploma?
Mario: No. Do I really need one?
Counselor: A GED can really help. A good mechanic needs to read instructions and manuals. Please think about it.
Mario: Thanks, I'm going to think about it.
CD 2, Track 50
6. Counselor: Nursing is a good job. You can take special classes at a university.
Marie: I already have plans to go to college here in town. Do I need to be a citizen?
Counselor: No, but you do need to be a state resident or it will cost you a lot of money.
Marie: Good. I am a state resident.

CD 2, Track 51, Page 150
B. Listen to the conversations. Check Exercise A.
1. Roberto: My name is Roberto. I am a student at Pine Adult School. I like to study and go to school. I think I would like to be a student for my whole life, but I know I will have to get a job someday. I love history so maybe I should look into being a teacher. I think that would be a great profession for me.
CD 2, Track 52
2. Eva: I love people. Every chance I get, I talk to people. They are so interesting. I like to help people. For that reason, I am going to choose a career that will enable me to be around people who I can help. I think being a nurse would be very rewarding. My mother is a nurse, too. It might be fun.
CD 2, Track 53
3. Duong: My name is Duong. I have a lot of experience working with my hands. I like to fix things, too. I love to make things work. That's why I think being a mechanic might be a good job for me. I like cars, too, so I think that this is a good choice.

CD 2, Track 54, Page 153
B. Look at the clocks. Then, listen to Nubar talk about his plans. Write what he is going to do next to the clocks. Use the phrases from the box.
I think that if I plan, I will be able to learn English well even when there is no school. I am going to read the newspaper, listen to the radio, and talk to people in English every day. Well, let's see. If I am going to do all this, I need to schedule these things. I will get home at 6:00 and then from 6:30 to 6:45 I will read the newspaper. I need to find time to study the textbook. I know—I will do that from 7:00 to 7:30. I will listen to the radio from 8:00 to 8:45. This should be good practice. During this time, I will review vocabulary, too. Then from 9:00 to 9:15, I will write in my journal. I am going to do this for a full month. Then, I will make new goals.

Photo Credits

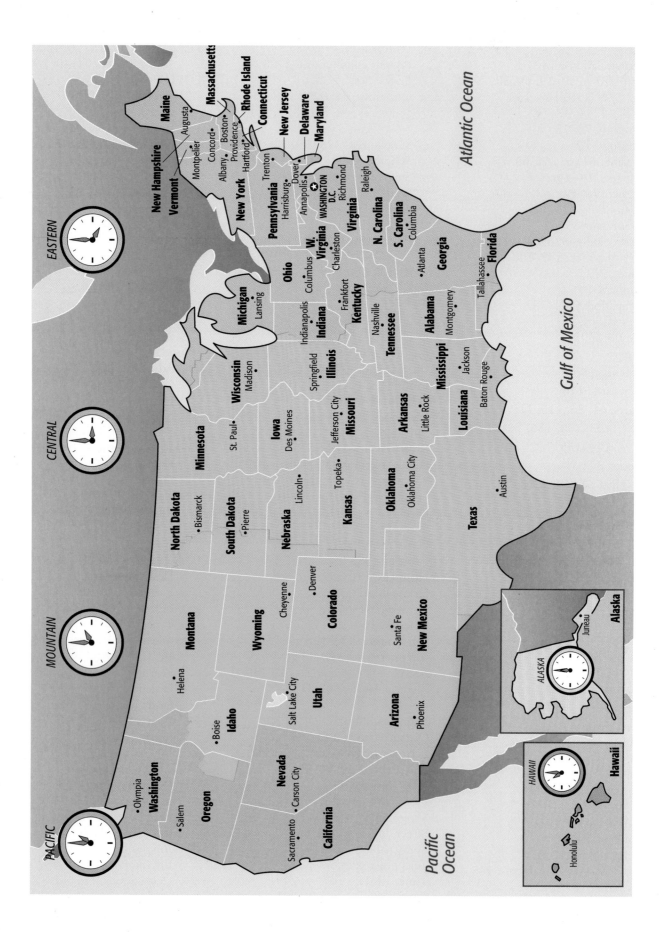

EASTERN

CENTRAL

MOUNTAIN

PACIFIC

Atlantic Ocean

Gulf of Mexico

Pacific Ocean

Maine
Augusta•

New Hampshire
Concord•
Montpelier•

Vermont

Massachusetts
Boston•

Rhode Island
Providence•

Connecticut
Hartford•

New York
Albany•

New Jersey
Trenton•

Delaware
Dover•

Maryland
Annapolis•

Pennsylvania
Harrisburg•

WASHINGTON D.C.

Virginia
Richmond•

W. Virginia
Charleston•

N. Carolina
Raleigh•

S. Carolina
Columbia•

Ohio
Columbus•

Indiana
Indianapolis•

Kentucky
Frankfort•

Tennessee
Nashville•

Georgia
Atlanta•

Florida
Tallahassee•

Michigan
Lansing•

Wisconsin
Madison•

Illinois
Springfield•

Missouri
Jefferson City•

Arkansas
Little Rock•

Alabama
Montgomery•

Mississippi
Jackson•

Louisiana
Baton Rouge•

Minnesota
St. Paul•

Iowa
Des Moines•

North Dakota
Bismarck•

South Dakota
Pierre•

Nebraska
Lincoln•

Kansas
Topeka•

Oklahoma
Oklahoma City•

Texas
Austin•

Montana
Helena•

Wyoming
Cheyenne•

Colorado
Denver•

New Mexico
Santa Fe•

Idaho
Boise•

Utah
Salt Lake City•

Arizona
Phoenix•

Washington
Olympia•

Oregon
Salem•

Nevada
Carson City•

California
Sacramento•

ALASKA
Alaska
Juneau•

HAWAII
Hawaii
Honolulu•

180   Map of the United States